David Picard, Sonja Buchberger (eds.)
Couchsurfing Cosmopolitanisms

Culture and Social Practice

David Picard, Sonja Buchberger (eds.)

Couchsurfing Cosmopolitanisms

Can Tourism Make a Better World?

[transcript]

Bibliographic information published by the Deutsche Nationalbibliothek
The Deutsche Nationalbibliothek lists this publication in the Deutsche Nationalbibliografie; detailed bibliographic data are available in the Internet at http://dnb.d-nb.de

Cover layout: Kordula Röckenhaus, Bielefeld
Cover illustration: ryu-tako / photocase.com
Typeset by Mark-Sebastian Schneider, Bielefeld
Printed and bound in Great Britain by Marston Book Services Ltd, Oxfordshire
ISBN 978-3-8376-2255-3

For the beautiful little barracuda

```
    .-^--.
)\/  (( o\
)/""----'
```

Content

1. Introduction: Couchsurfing in Lisbon, Tunis and Brisbane

David Picard and Sonja Buchberger

At the home of strangers: couchsurfing in Lisbon (David Picard)[1]

One day in early June 2009, Clara[2] was occupied with the preparation of a promotional event that her employer, a national communication agency, was organising. She left the office well after 8pm, and I met her at the entrance to the train station. She had rich brown hair; she was tanned and slim. She looked straight at me with an open smile. I found her very attractive. After kissing hello, we walked to her apartment, a couple of hundred metres from the station. We spoke in English about Lisbon, about my trip there and about her current work project. I told her that I had been offered a research job, and wanted to visit the city to see what the environment and my colleagues would be like. I had spent the first day walking around town, and had also met my potential line manager. She could not say anything more specific about the job, and recommended I meet the head of department of the university where I was to be hosted the next day.

---

1 | We would like to thank Nelson Graburn and Tamas Régi for their helpful comments on the introduction. Special thanks go to Jeremy Lowe for his thorough proof-reading of the book draft, and to the production team of *transcipt*, our publisher, for their efficiency and friendliness. The work invested into the editing of this book was partly financed through national funds provided by the Portuguese Foundation for Science and Technology (FCT), Project PTDC/CS-ANT/114825/2009.

2 | All names of couchsurfers in this chapter are replaced by pseudonyms.

Clara suggested that we have grilled sardines and potatoes in a fairground a couple of minutes' walk from her house. Lisbon was in the festive period, she explained, and going to the fairground was what people tended to do. The fairground was built in a valley near the train station. The different stands were selling lots of different things – sweets, bread, grilled food, bags, cloth and exotic handicraft products. Half a dozen stalls selling grilled sardines and potatoes were arranged in a large circle at the furthest end. Music came from loudspeakers, and a couple of children were dancing on an improvised stage. We were sitting down on white plastic chairs at a white plastic table. Clara ordered a dozen sardines, boiled potatoes and beer. Our conversation turned to memories of past travel, countries we had visited and projects for the future. Clara had been volunteering in a primary school in Mozambique three years before. The experience had transformed her, she said. She had realised that she could not take her life and commodities for granted.

I had met Clara through Couchsurfing.org, an online hospitality community site that allows its members to offer their "couch" or guest bedroom to other members and, vice and versa, to contact members in other places to request their hospitality. I had learnt about the site through a friend in England, and had used it for the first time. Before sending Clara an official "couch request", I had spent quite a lot of time browsing through the profiles of different members in the Lisbon area, checking their preferences, their jobs, their age, their travel experiences, their interests and their "mission" in life. On her profile page, Clara had declared that she was "still looking for [a mission] ... Can you help?" There was further information: about her profession, language skills, interests and past travels. I had thought that we were somehow compatible, and I added her to my "favourites". I created my own profile page and sent her a message requesting to "surf" her couch for a couple of days. I explained that I was working as an anthropologist at a university in England, and that I was to visit Lisbon for this length of time. I told her that I had never been in Lisbon before; neither had I been to Cuba or China (I had learnt from her profile page that she had travelled to these countries), but that I knew Madagascar and Reunion Island quite well. I also told her that this was my first couchsurfing experience, that I spoke English, French and German, and that I would be happy to meet her, exchange ideas and stay at her place. Two days later she replied, saying that she'd be happy to offer hospitality and also make suggestions of things to do to discover the city. She had pasted her mobile phone number in the message, and proposed to meet up at the train station on the evening of the day of my arrival.

That night, after dinner, we went back to her place. I asked her about Fado music, which was about the only thing I "knew" about Portugal. She liked Fado, she said. She had a large collection of CDs in her living room, and later played some of them, telling me stories about the different singers. I told her about my affection for the music of Madredeus, a Portuguese band that had been featured in a 1990s film by Wim Wenders called *Lisbon Story*. I liked the tonality of the voice and the guitar music. For a couple of years I had had a tape by the band, which I frequently played at home. I thought that Madredeus's music sympathetically translated the plot of the Wim Wenders movie into the realm of sound. The film was about two German filmmakers existentially trying to capture what they conceived of as unconditional beauty. The old town of Lisbon, with its popular quarters, bright sun light and yellow tram carriages, is used as the visual backdrop for this quest, and for the movie itself. In the film, one of the filmmakers, a sound engineer, is tantalised by the subtle reverberations of the city and the beauty of the voice of a woman he meets in his neighbourhood (the then lead singer of Madredeus, Teresa Salgueiro). The other filmmaker, frustrated by his hopeless quest for absolute beauty, has by then disappeared into the city. Both filmmakers eventually find each other once again and conclude that, while there is no unconditional beauty to be discovered out there (all beauty is created in the human mind, they realise), one can still have a lot of fun chasing the idea. The film ends with the two filmmakers using a hand-operated camera to shoot scenes of the enigmatic yellow tram driving through the winding streets of Lisbon's old town. At the time, it was one of my favourite movies and plots. But Clara said that, although Madredeus was nice, it was not really the original Fado. She later gave me bed sheets and opened the fold-up sofa in her living room. She also left me a pair of keys so that I could get into the house during the following days.

The copy of the work contract I received during my meeting the following day contained the heading "of uncertain duration". The head of department convinced me that this was just a formality and that I was not to worry, that there were no problems. The job was paid much less than the one I had in England, and I was not sure if I should sign. My friends and colleagues back in England had warned me not to give up my tenured position there.

I eventually stayed at Clara's house for two more nights. We spent a considerable amount of time together, talking, cooking, listening to music, going out, watching a movie and meeting her friends for a barbecue. During the day I walked aimlessly around Lisbon, discovering some of its neighbourhoods. I did not find the city and ambience depicted in Wim Wenders' film. All looked fairly run down. The walls were full of graffiti, many houses were in ruin and there was rubbish in the streets. I found that many people looked unhappy; they talked in low voices, avoiding eye contact, and many had deep wrinkles around their mouths. The sofa-bed at Clara's place was uncomfortable, and my back hurt. But I liked her company and our conversations about the world, and about what we would do in life. She firmly believed in God. I was intrigued by this religious conviction, and maybe even more by her generous hospitality. I asked her if she was not scared to let strangers stay at her house and leave them with the keys. She wasn't, she said: people return the trust and confidences they are offered. Or at least she hoped so. She smiled when she said that. After returning to England, I wrote her a "positive" reference, which appeared on her couchsurfing profile page. I wrote, "Clara was the first person who ever hosted me via this network, and if all couchsurfers are like her, I predict the near end of capitalism as a way to organise human relations; a new era of transhumance based on kindness, trust, friendliness, and, of course, grilled sardines. I still smell like [a] dog, feel my back ache, and am unsure about my faith in materialism; Clara will transform you. Be nice to her". She reciprocated with a "positive" reference, writing that, "David has a life history that makes envy to any human being! I hope one day you can hear it, and see the film he produced. As a 'surfer', I only can praise [him]: always [in a] good mood (he had even lunched with my crazy friends and a crazy dog, always with a smile). A very interesting, intelligent, focused and funny person. Until September, David!"

I had been looking forward to living and working in a sunnier place, and I signed the contract some days later. I started the new post in September 2009.

Investigating Couchsurfing Culture

Since the early 2000s, the emergence of computer-mediated communication and online hospitality community platforms has transformed many accustomed practices of doing tourism and organising hospitality. Instead of booking packaged tours and accommodation through a travel agent, many travellers have started to create direct contact with possible hosts, travel companions or local guides. At the same time, private hosts are increasingly able to open their homes to what were once total strangers from around the world, integrate them into the spaces of their everyday lives and, often, also earn considerable sums of money by renting out rooms or private apartments. In this new digital era, in order to prepare the logistics of the journey both hosts and guests initially interact within the online environment and then meet up, hang out and even host each other in the offline context of actual travel. Cutting out most of the traditional professional tourism and travel agents, computer-mediated hospitality generates new realms of hospitality and tourism where hosts and guests interact directly, in private and, in many cases, outside the de facto reach of any publicly sanctioned governing body, chamber of commerce or other means of control[3]. Why and how does it work? Why would people let complete strangers stay at their houses, often leaving them with the keys and not charging them a penny? What is the ideological force driving such practices, and what forms of social relations and society do they bring about in the contemporary world? Does the popularity of couchsurfing indicate the near end of capitalism, giving rise to new forms of organising human relations?

To this date, academic research attempting to explore these questions is only about to emerge. Some recent contributions include a special issue of *Hospitality & Society* edited by Jennie Germann Molz (2011) and two monographs by Paula Bialski (2007, 2012). The aim of this book is to provide fresh data from a greater range of ethnographic settings in which online-to-offline hospitality exchanges take place. To achieve this aim, the contributors focus in particular on travel and hospitality practices that have evolved within and around the online hospitality community site Couchsurfing.org. This has become one of the internationally most visible and – with

3 | Commercial hospitality community websites such as AIRBNB strongly recommend that their members respect the national legislations of the countries in which they live, especially with regard to tax regulations for short-term rentals. However, for national and local tax agencies, it is usually technically difficult and economically hardly viable to trace the large amount of relatively low private-to-private payments made in the online-to-offline hospitality community sector. In the USA, the professional hotel and hospitality sectors increasingly accuse sites like AIRBNB of encouraging tax evasion and flouting local regulations on short-term rentals. The controversy is on-going at the time of writing this book.

more than 4 million members worldwide – also one of the most successful online hospitality community sites. Because it imposes as its principal rule that hospitality be granted free of charge, it is, in a way, also one of the most "extreme" sites of its type. Couchsurfing.org's operational premise is that the exchanges between hosts and guests take place outside the realms of commercial tourism transactions, a stipulation which – so it is claimed by the site owners – constitutes a basic condition for promoting "a world where everyone can explore and create meaningful connections with the people and places we encounter" (Couchsurfing.org, 2012). Until a recent legal status upgrade that transformed its formerly tax exempt, not-for-profit status and turned it into a more operational – and potentially profit-generating – business corporation, the site's official slogan was to "create a better world, one couch at a time". Even after this update, the core mission of the site remains structured around the objective of generating intercultural exchange and learning, "to explore, learn and grow" – ultimately as a means to create a "better world". For a social scientist, this stated objective, and the suggestion that travel and hospitality are the means to achieve it, provokes a number of exciting interrogations. Why and how would travel and hospitality create a "better world"? What defines the extensions and internal structure of such a "world"? And what defines its "betterment"?

To explore these questions, the authors of this book employ different approaches and methods; many – including ourselves – using their own experiences as hosts, guests and community organisers to feed their analysis. Most use a combined approach focused on couchsurfing contexts and practices that are evolving both offline and online. Their "insider" position as active couchsurfers has allowed many to draw extensively on the ethnographic method of participant observation, which seems the natural choice to study one's "own" culture (Powdermaker, 1966; Okely, 1996). Sonja Buchberger (Chapter 4) spent some years in Tunis in Tunisia, first as a university student and then as a PhD researcher investigating narratives and practices of couchsurfing among various members of the local couchsurfing community. Jun-E Tan (Chapter 7) spent a three-year period investigating couchsurfing practices in Singapore and other places, hosting couchsurfers on 50 occasions and surfing herself 28 times. Similarly, Bernard Schéou (Chapter 6) participated actively in the local couchsurfing community in Ho Chi Minh City in Vietnam, observing the relation between the global couchsurfing format and localised cultures of gender and domestic hospitality. Using his own hosting experiences, Dennis Zuev (Chapter 3), who grew up in Siberia, investigates the host position from an insider's perspective. In an autobiographical study on his and his family's experiences hosting (mainly Western) couchsurfing travellers, he explores the frictions between couchsurfing practice and Siberian hospitality culture. Having been an early member of the couchsurfing movement herself, and having actively participated in the development of the community, Paula Bialski (Chapter 8) reflects on her involvement and describes how couchsurfing grew into one of the most prominent online-offline communities worldwide. Most authors combine their direct observations with more systematic approaches to the general contexts in which couchsurfing evolves, variably using historical analysis, questionnaires and interviews with targeted samples. Paula Bialski carried out a large-scale survey to study motivations to join and participate in the community, which was integrated as a feature within the couchsurfing site. To investigate the cosmopolitan imaginings that Taiwanese couchsurfers associate with couchsurfing practice, De Jung Chen organised group workshops with members and actively participated in dedicated couchsurfing discussion boards based on shared interests.

The online environment usually facilitated these study approaches. Many interviews and surveys were carried out online using Internet telephone technology, online survey technologies and databases extracted from the publicly available information users provide online. Those researchers who investigated specific localised couchsurfing communities – Sonja Buchberger in Tunisia, Dennis Zuev in Siberia, Bernard Schéou in Vietnam, De-Jung Chen in Taiwan – computed the information that couchsurfers made available in their profiles to delimit their samples and qualitatively analyse common social, sociological and lifestyle patterns among their respective samples. This methodological strategy allowed them, for instance, to categorise their samples according to criteria such as language ability, travel experiences, age, gender and education. Most authors note an analytic ambivalence they were confronted with when analysing the meanings of specific online performances by couchsurfing members. It was usually not clear whether – say – the "mission statement" or "philosophy" an individual couchsurfer advertised on their profile page, or their participation in publicly visible chat rooms, were to be approached in terms of texts or interactions (cf. Hine, 2000:53f.). While there is an obvious co-presence of the parties involved in the rhetorical performances of public self-representation and the exchanges of publicly visible messages, there was still a separation in space and, to a lesser degree, in time. The authors in this book have generally adopted one of two possible strategies. Tan and Buchberger applied ethnographic approaches of participant observation in forum discussions by posting themselves, and thus getting actively involved, whereas Chen, Germann Molz and Schéou used approaches based on discourse analysis to understand such performances in terms of texts.

Participant observation in and of a largely open-ended online community elicits a number of ethical dilemmas. It is far from guaranteed that all subjects investigated here were aware of the presence of researchers or had the opportunity to give – or refuse – their prior informed consent. Moreover, despite "protecting" their informants through the use of pseudonyms, all authors have publicly visible couchsurfing profiles that lead relatively easily to the proper identities of many interlocutors.

Several of the chapters in this book are based on the authors' personal experiences as friends, researchers, tourists and travel companions. Many have been the guests of their research participants, which seems an ideal situation to observe hospitality practice as it unfolds in a normal setting. As Candea and da Col put it, hospitality is "the unavoidable condition of possibility of ethnography" (Candea and da Col, 2012:3). In most study contexts, the ethnographer is, and mainly remains, a stranger, and observes social reality from within this specific perspective. In the first stages of ethnographic work, what is usually observed is merely the persona adopted to charm or contain the stranger and check up on his or her intentions. The ethnographic strategy of progressively becoming an insider thus implies a process of becoming a more and more intimate stranger, seen from the perspective of locals (Picard, 2011). Being active couchsurfers themselves helped the authors of the book to access the field, because it provided them with an "operational" identity and a role they were expected to fulfil. Like all other couchsurfers, they had to "fit in" and face the challenges of interaction.

The methodological strategy to explore couchsurfing by adopting the role of the guest came with other inherent paradoxes, such as the constant bordering as the figure of the parasite – the unwelcome guest – challenging the sovereignty of the hosts by potentially taking more than giving back. The ethnography of couchsurfing therefore was in many ways a constant walk on the borderline, where it was not certain if the expectations of host and guest would be met or thwarted. Most authors used the relative fluidity of this situation to their advantage, to explore how the global narratives of the couchsurfing project were met and adapted to various local contexts, and to test the "solidity" of the social and moral structures governing the phenomenon.

Tourism, cosmopolitanism and modern culture

The first and most obvious observation made by the authors of the book is that the practice and – as we shall see – underlying cosmopolitan ideology of couchsurfing pertains to a very significant degree to "modern culture". The quasi-totality of the network's members – called "couchsurfers" – is located in Europe, the Americas or Australia. Less than 10 % reside in Asia (cf. Schéou, Chapter 6; Chen, Chapter 5). Couchsurfers are generally relatively well-educated, highly media-literate and proficient in navigating Internet websites (Bialski, Chapter 8). And they are relatively young – on average 27. Most speak several languages, and many have significant overseas travel experience. While the average couchsurfer has one couchsurfing experience per year, a hard-core of members practice couchsurfing – as host, guest or organiser of events – very frequently, often with several couchsurfing contacts per week. In this sense, the world the couchsurfing project brings into being is that of a relatively young, mainly Western, transnational middle class, with a minimum level of economic means and access to technology and international travel visas.

What brings these couchsurfers together seems to be a widely shared culture and passion for travel and the encountering of "Others". Couchsurfing creates its own realms, and what has elsewhere been called cosmopolitan "ambiances" (Beck, 2006) and consumption practices (cf. Germann Molz, 2011). It operates in an often ambiguous and highly politicised social field marked by philosophical debates on what it means to be human (Appiah, 2006; Amit and Rapport, 2012; Rapport, 2012), how to govern world society (Dower, 2003) and which forms of sociability and social inclusions and exclusions structure the global world (Forte, 2010; Werbner, 2008). De-Jung Chen (Chapter 5), in her chapter on Taiwanese couchsurfers, argues that the emergence of cosmopolitan realms and ambiances is governed by a specific knowledge based on cultural stereotypes and conventionalised ways of dealing with difference that emanate from the Western world. She stresses that learning of stereotypes of various Others, including an exoticised Self, becomes a key for many Taiwanese surfers to participate in what they perceive as an urban global modernity. While claiming to overcome cultural differences through the encounters made during the journey, Chen suggests that couchsurfing – like most tourism practices in general (cf. Laxton, 1991) – instead candidly reinforces cultural stereotypes and a specific regime of representing and organising global cultural diversity.

Similarly, various authors working in the field of anthropological studies of tourism argue that the tour is a socially institutionalised, highly ceremonialised means to leave the familiarity of home and proactively go on a quest for an exotic Other (Löfgren, 2002). The tour and the realms encountered during the tour are framed by powerful meta-narratives (Bruner, 2005) or "modern myths" (MacCannell, 1976; Selwyn, 1996) that lead the travellers to the locales of their adventures, and that also provide them with story elements and images to make sense of the emotions and personal experiences made during the tour (Picard and Robinson, 2012). In this sense, the exotic is not an open concept, but is framed within a specific culture of expectations, associations and collective gazes (Urry, 2002). Specific people and places generally stand, here, for particular exotic realms formed within the collective mind-sets of modernist thinking. East African Pygmies, Australian Aboriginals or Alaskan American-Indians, for example, often stand for a wider imaginary of the primitive and pristine – seemingly perpetuating the 19th-century social taxonomies and racist fantasy hierarchies brought about by evolutionist ideology (Frankland, 2009). By suggesting that certain people or places represent an earlier stage of evolution, or a possible alternative to the disenchantments brought about by modernity, such ideas of the primitive become part of a powerful, explicit meta-narrative of modern time and being (Picard, 2011). The history of nature and humanity becomes embedded here within a specific "logic" and underlying moral (in Western terms, Christian) rationale. In the beginning there was almost nothing: a pristine, unconditioned nature which was subsequently populated by small-scale populations living in harmony. The imaginary realm depicted in the biblical book of Genesis arguably remains the single most influential reference for defining and qualifying this earliest realm. For the moderns, the purity of biblical nature is periodically rediscovered through the enjoyment of beaches, mountains, lakes, rivers, forests, gardens and deserts encountered during holidays and other work-life breaks. In much of modern culture, this imaginary, unspoilt realm also marks a symbolic departure point for the course of human development. Following the biblical metaphor of the loss of Eden, history is initiated as a consequence of human action and freewill; humanity stands up against the unconditionality of divine nature, beauty and perfection, and forms society according to its own ideals. Adam and Eve leave Paradise after their famous act of luscious self-determination – eating from the tree of wisdom and becoming wise like God herself. The subsequent history of humanity is then narrated mainly through events of great discovery, great artistic, architectural and technological achievements and, also, great violence and wars.

Here again, particular people and places are made to stand for such specific events inscribed in the historical imagination of modernist thinking. Remnants of past "great civilisations" – Chinese, Egyptian, Greek, Roman and Arab, for example – generate narratives of imagined filiation and cultural ancestry (Sahlins, 1993), usually without regard for the current social and cultural realities in the places in which these remnants are found. Other "great" civilisations – like the Inka or the Maya – provide allegorical grounds to tell stories of human genius, and also supply metaphors for thinking about empire and globalisation in more general terms. Accordingly, at least since the European Renaissance, modernity has thus fashioned itself within a globally extended, theatrical realm of social life (Greenblatt, 1980), where forms of invocation, contact and travel allow the moderns to playfully engage and ceremonially renew the specific plots and social roles of this world history play. In this sense, exotic Others are always related to a modern Self. The city of Lisbon and the touristically adapted Fado music dramatised in the Wim Wenders film mentioned above supply a specific image of, and realm in which to encounter, such an exotic Other. The plot is driven by a biblical quest for unconditional beauty, and eventually leads the "touristic" heroes to realise the relativity of beauty as a fantasy world that merely exists in their minds, but which is still fun to chase and bring to life.

Tourism – like cinema – thus creates its own realms which integrate "destinations" into a wider social world. The recent ethnographic works on tourism contact zones in Southern Ethiopia (Régi, 2012), Tanzania and Indonesia (Salazar, 2010) and La Réunion (Picard, 2010) show how the learning and performing of cultural stereotypes projected upon local populations by outside tourists become means for these populations to participate in the "cosmopolitan" realms of a wider, global world. The "vernacular" (Werbner, 2008) cosmopolitanisms respectively developed in these cases by the Ethiopian Mursi, the Tanzanian and Indonesian tour guides and the socially marginal populations of La Réunion respond to tourist demand and a more general imaginary of the past, the local and the exotic or the futuristic (in the case of La Réunion's Creoles), anchored in modern culture and culture polity. Similarly, the Fado mentioned earlier, hitherto associated by many local intellectuals and activists in Portugal with the luso-romanticism institutionalised by the country's former fascist regime, becomes "sexy" once again through the touristic eye and the related classification on UNESCO's list of intangible heritage. World citizenship, as the conviction that people from all over the world are part of a universal human history, is in these cases not based on a principle of equality, but of attributed social difference and theatrically performed exotic otherness. Paradoxically, performing the social role of the exotic Other becomes here a specific means for non-Western populations to be cosmopolite.

Candid Hospitality and the Betterment of the World

Couchsurfing claims to push tourism to another level as it cuts out the various commercial and professional intermediaries, travel agents and tour operators who would ordinarily organise tours and prescribe what to visit. Because they are enabled to access the social intimacy of hosts and their friends and families, couchsurfers often argue that they break out of the structural confines that keep "ordinary" tourists prisoners of their own expectations and therefore enable "truly" "authentic" and "meaningful" experiences. Couchsurfers often assert that they do not know what will happen once they enter the house of a host. They usually maintain that their form of tourism is not solely about the traveller, but about the contact and exchange created between host and guest. Couchsurfing in this sense is about access to social intimacy and the (usually) unseen cultural; access to realms that are – so the couchsurfers seem to believe – ontologically more "real" than the presumed "artifice" of staged tourism settings. The Couchsurfing website thus cultivates a utopian rhetoric of "sharing cultures", of increased and rapid interconnections and global flows of all kinds. People are just not "aware" of these elements, as the Couchsurfing.org slogan, "The world is smaller than you think", seems to imply. The "surfing of couches", then, is depicted as a fun mode of practice to increase this awareness.

In large parts, the organisation reiterates ideologies found in most other forms of tourism practice. It might be read as yet another materialisation of what Butcher (2003) terms the "moralisation" of modern leisure travel, with contemporary travellers being preoccupied with ethical claims, personal growth and the exploration of both self and of new "peripheral" places. Lanfant and Graburn (1992) argue that this particular ideology was in a much larger context formative for the 1960s "alternative movements" in Germany and the USA. By rejecting consumer culture and, by extension, mass tourism as something "fake", these movements, Lanfant and Graburn suggest, set the basis for new discourses and concepts regarding "alternative" forms of tourism. The latter, it is often claimed, are founded on principles of equality of exchange, respect for the cultural integrity and authenticity of the visited, and the sustainable use of resources by the tourism sector. The same principles resurface as an ethical backbone in the couchsurfing project. Where hosts and guests become considered equals, citizens of a same world, the moral and ontological boundary between them becomes blurred.

Couchsurfing thus provides a narrative to qualify the global world it has set out to create and the means by which it is to be achieved. The "better" in "creating a better world" defines a process of social and moral transformation that the act of couchsurfing is to realise. Humanity is to move towards an ideal society of the future in which diversity is approached with "curiosity, appreciation and respect" (Couchsurfing.org, 2012). What also seems to re-emerge here and in other alternative tourism movements is the influential political philosophy of Immanuel Kant, which, since its formulation in the late-18th century, has marked all major political debates in the Western world about global governance and peace (Dowdeswell, 2011). In 1795, Kant suggested that "universal hospitality" was a condition for the creation of a world of "perpetual peace". He explained that the "right of a stranger not to be treated as an enemy when he [or she] arrives in the land of another" would allow "the human race [to] gradually be brought closer and closer to a constitution establishing world citizenship". Kant's philosophical thinking had a lasting influence on subsequent philosophers and state philosophies, and also flowed into the wider common understanding of Western culture. A prominent thinker who picked up on Kant's ideas was the French philosopher and political activist Jacques Derrida, who proposed a hyperbolic notion of "absolute hospitality", according to which strangers are actively welcomed without consideration of who they are, where they come from, how much money they have or how much prestige they can confer. While in Kant's understanding of hospitality strangers should not be harmed, and must be offered protection until they move on (because they are presumed to move on), Derrida pushes the stakes higher, making hospitality not only a right to be enjoyed by strangers, but an impossible, unconditional moral ideal to guide interpersonal relations among humans in general (Derrida, 2000). The claims made by Derrida's political philosophy often come up in contemporary debates on how to "deal" with illicit immigrants in Western countries (Friese, 2009; Lenz, 2010; Rosello, 2001; Still, 2010). One common argument brought forward by the "alternative" movements is that if pure human solidarity is an end in itself, the notion of strangers and the underlying ontology of borders between humans no longer make sense.

In these discourses, the concept of boundaries is usually associated with that of "interest", which itself is normally considered via a distinction between somehow "inauthentic" commercial and "real" human interests. Kant explained that to make a "better" world and be "truly" human, one must "do good", which for him was defined by selflessly non-interested and, in particular, non-commercial acts. Kant illustrated his understanding of doing good through a negative example. In his 1795 text on perpetual peace, he decried the injustices – exploitation of resources, enslavement of people and indebtedness of foreign economies – committed by the European colonial states. In particular, he despised situations where commercially or politically interested actions mobilise humanity to further their ends, rather than treating humanity as an end in itself. Kant wrote with particular disgust about the English as a "commercial people" who, by means of economic exploitation and political despotism, subjugated the world to their rule. Kant's argument that only non-commercial relations between people are morally "good" became a central maxim of the alternative movements. Implying that commercial relations automatically generate meaningless acts, many proponents of these alternative movements, including prominent intellectuals like Walter Benjamin, seemed to believe in a form of natural magic or "aura" that inhabits objects and human relations, and which disappears whenever money is introduced into the games of exchange.

Yet, it seems to us that what defines what is and what isn't a commercial relation is essentially subject to narratives and ideology. In the field of tourism, tourists do not, in practice, "buy" experiences or "consume" places. Such formulations are part of narratives about tourism employed by developers, businessmen and pessimist sociologists, but usually not by tourists themselves. Certainly, the expenditure of economic wealth in the form of money takes place in the wider framework of tourism practice. Tourists – like all social actors engaging in social relations with others – pay to balance a form of expected reciprocity. Paying in the form of monetary exchanges, gift-giving, sacrifice or respect and recognition is part of the touristic play (Graburn, 1983). Following this observation, a number of authors have started to study – and reconsider – the structure and meaning of hospitality practices that emerge in different more or less commercialised hospitality settings (Heal, 1990; Lashley and Morrison, 2001; Lashley, Lynch and Morrison, 2007). Studies on ordinary mass-tourists by Wang (2000), Picard (2011) and Crossley (2012) demonstrate that the mass-produced sites and products that seem to be meaninglessly "bought" and "consumed" by tourists do actually generate meaningful and often deeply transformative experiences among tourists.

What seems to drive the debates among "alternative" tourists and academics about the meaningfulness or meaninglessness of other people's experiences is an age-old need for social distinction, observed to have already pertained among imperial Roman holidaymakers 2000 years ago, when competing over who was having the more "real" Greek lifestyle performance-experience (Feifer, 1985). Then and now, each class of tourist claims that its respective forms of tourism and the experiences it has are superior (Adler, 1989). Like a caricature of social relations back home, Antarctic deep-time geologists feel superior to anthropologists while on their tours, who in turn feel superior to travel journalists, who feel superior to backpackers, who feel superior to mass-tourists (Cohen, 2004).

To ensure that they are not associated with the narratives of commerce and the related suspicion of superficial, inauthentic experiences and conspicuous consumption, alternative tourism movements like couchsurfing simply take the transfer of money out of their practice, or hide it where possible. By rejecting any form of commercial transaction, couchsurfers take the most extreme position with regard to this ideology. Hospitality among members remains free, and ought to be commercially disinterested; it is above all about meeting people, learning and making a better world. It is not about "consuming", but about "learning" and "growing".

The argument that because hospitality is free it inherently allows couchsurfers to take "cheap" holidays is actively refuted by large parts of the couchsurfing movement (as the chapters in this book discuss). Hospitality is, above all, seen as a means to achieve something different: "honest" hospitality and a "real" interest in others. It is candid because it implies an act that is carried out in a naïve but full belief in its inherent goodness, or at least the goodness of its consequences. Candid hospitality is driven by convictions about its intrinsic potential to create a better world. In this way, couchsurfing puts the Western philosophical notion of "true" humanity in a "let's-do-it" way into practice.

While the rhetoric of hospitality and the betterment of the world is frequently mobilised by couchsurfers and the couchsurfing project, in practice the reality is relatively far from such notions as Derrida's "absolute hospitality". Hospitality is, in most cases, not a right to be unconditionally enjoyed by strangers but, at best, a right to be requested by travellers, refugees or migrants (Germann Molz, Chapter 2). At a macro-level, the hospitality offered through couchsurfing is conditioned by international visa agreements, access to economic resources, computer literacy and the ability to generate trust among fellow surfers. The couchsurfing website allows members to create profile pages on which they can – naïvely or strategically – place signs and symbols to generate trust. Tan (Chapter 7) argues that information about language skills, previous travel experience, personal interests and knowledge of online "taboos" are cultural capitals that allow couchsurfers to advertise their inclusion in an in-group of global cosmopolites. Whoever does not possess such "cultural capital", and who therefore is not able to provide such signifiers of inclusion and understanding of the wider "project", or who grossly misunderstands the often humoristic undertone of the couchsurfers' self-declared "mission statements", will have far more difficulty in using the website to make friends and generate contact experiences. Considering its ideological frame and sociological constraints, it therefore seems that the couchsurfing project brings together, above all, a global middle-class of mainly younger people from mainly Western countries claiming to be advocates for a generalised "humanity". Yet, the "world" that couchsurfers and other Western tourists refer to is formulated and formed to a large extent within the centres of Western societies. Just like in other forms of tourism, public representations, maps and stories here become tools to transform other people and places into a global sphere of attractions.

At the same time, far from being passive "victims" of a presumably cannibalistic global tourism system, these "local" people often become proactive players themselves, taking on the role of hosts and increasingly becoming travellers themselves (Bruner, 2005). In many contexts, couchsurfing represents a specific form of "sexy" urban global modernity in which young, aspiring people from non-Western countries want to take part (Schéou, Chapter 6). Chen (Chapter 5) demonstrates that, while for most Westerners cosmopolitanism represents a world-encompassing philosophy, for Taiwanese surfers (for example) it is a specific means to participate in a global urban modernity. Cosmopolitanism is learnt here through repetitions, like one would learn a language or an instrument; once acquired, its techniques and knowledge allow the Taiwanese surfers to navigate the global, modern world. The learning process reveals the inner contradictions of the couchsurfing movement: it claims equality and transparency, yet – in the understanding of the Taiwanese at least – is based on a complex set of cultural stereotypes projected in the imagined geographies of the world, which eventually perpetuate discriminations and differences. Drawing on her work on alternate norms of hospitality that govern relations to strangers among couchsurfing hosts in Tunis, Tunisia, Sonja Buchberger shows (in the next section) how contact with Western cosmopolite travel culture can lead to the emergence of localised "rooted" or "vernacular" cosmopolitanisms (Swain, 2001; Werbner, 2008). The story of Mehmet supplies here an entry to explore this issue.

Deceived kinship and the formation of vernacular cosmopolitanisms in Tunisia (Sonja Buchberger)

Mehmet had joined us at the weekly gathering of the couchsurfing community in Tunis. He was from Turkey, and had been on a three-week trip through Italy, Spain and Tunisia. He explained to me that he had brought gifts from Turkey for the hosts that he would meet on the way. All these gifts he had stored in his only luggage, a backpack that seemed so full that I thought it would burst open at any moment. He said that he had brought Turkish coffee, little cotton bags, Turkish delight and other souvenirs. Mehmet told me that while he had been travelling through Europe he had not felt well-received. He said that many of his hosts had been "unthankful" and did "not do anything for [him]". He also stressed that he had had to send many "couch requests" before eventually finding a host who accepted him into their home. He speculated that the reason for this was that Europeans liked to use the couchsurfing network to travel abroad and find hosts in other countries, but not to host foreigners in their own homes once they returned from their travels. He wondered if any of the European couchsurfers he had hosted in his home in Turkey would, in turn, host him at their places in Europe. The Tunisian couchsurfers who had arrived were attentively listening in on our conversation. Mehmet, now centre of attention, continued his story. He complained that his European guests had not offered him any gifts as a sign of gratitude for his hospitality. The meetings of the Tunis couchsurfing community habitually took place in a renovated grand house in the city's old town. Young Tunisian business-people had turned the building into a "cultural café" decorated with modern Tunisian paintings on the walls; they ran a book sale and organised regular jazz evenings.

That night, after listening to Mehmet's story, a heated discussion unfolded among the Tunisian members of the network. Most agreed with his complaints; many started to tell their own stories of exploited and unreciprocated hospitality. Some of those present who had never travelled abroad questioned whether they would find any hosts when travelling in Europe, asking if they would not be subjected to "discrimination" and "racism" against Arabs. Mehmet concluded that for him there were many similarities between Tunisian and Turkish hospitality. All seemed to agree once again.What was at stake here for the Tunisian couchsurfing members was not only the "consumption" of cosmopolitanism, which is much discussed in the literature. While the Tunisian participants largely shared practices such as watching satellite TV, buying low-priced Chinese products from the souk or wearing fake Levis jeans with many people outside of the network, what set their understandings apart was their stress on the importance of "friendship" in the way they engaged with "the wider world". According to the couchsurfing ideal, members are driven by the strong will and conscious decision to engage with real individuals from abroad – most often not only to chat with them online, but to meet them face-to-face, host them and become "friends", maybe even lovers. In studies on urban imageries and processes of "branding" cities as cosmopolitan, it has been held that such "cosmopolitan" cities cannot simply turn inhabitants into cosmopolitans (Binnie et al., 2006; Donald, Kevin and Kofman, 2009; Diep, Drabble and Young, 2006). In a similar way, participation in a "cosmopolitan network" does not make all of the people involved enthusiastic followers of the same understanding of cosmopolitanism. Rather, what is required is to explore the range of meanings that (in this case) the Tunisian users attached to cosmopolitanism. Clearly, many of my research participants mobilised the narrative of cosmopolitanism as a framework to express their thoughts. Departing from the assumption that the relationship between the local and the cosmopolitan is highly complex, I had started to explore the ways in which "individual and collective actors in the postcolonial world make that world by engaging with each other and with cosmopolitan ideas and movements beyond their immediate locales" (Werbner, 2008:8).

I had been living and studying in Tunis since the early 2000s, and had grown used to discussions about cosmopolitanism and the idea that Westerners were hostile towards Arab people. The topic regularly came up in small-talk conversations, for instance when I was getting to know someone new. Arguably, the most common question I was confronted with here was what I thought about Islam. I was asked if I did not regard all Muslims to be "terrorists", or if my parents were not afraid about me travelling to a "Muslim country". What was usually required was a long and arduous development of trust, in which I had to stress the absence of any negative feelings from my side. Many of my friends thought that Westerners were afraid of Muslims, and so felt rejected. A 17-year-old pupil and cousin of a friend from the Tunisian city of Sousse, for instance, was moved to tears when I managed to convince her that I was genuinely "unafraid" of Muslims and that I did not "reject" her. A long-standing friend in his 30s who was trying to make a living in the film industry often said that he "would like to hug" all those foreign students of Arabic language in the Bourguiba school, Tunis. What impressed him was their commitment to learn the language: a commitment which, it seemed to him, attested to their intention to approach Arab culture with an attitude of genuine interest and empathy.

Similar ambiguities were also obvious in the relations that I developed with lecturers during my studies at the University of Tunis. Some referred to the American sociologist Samuel Huntington as the most influential contemporary thinker of "the West". In the early 1990s, Samuel Huntington had written his influential monograph *The Clash of Civilizations and the Remaking of World Order* (1996) on the future configuration of the world political order. He predicted a coming "clash of civilizations" – in particular between what he defined as the Christian West and the Muslim Arab world. Huntington's thesis had a major influence on American foreign policy throughout the 1990s, providing an ideological base for George W. Bush's later "War on Terror". My lecturers in Tunis often seemed to imply that Huntington's ideas were uncritically taught at Western universities, thus disseminating and normalising a specific vision of the relations between Western and Arab countries among Western students.

What Mehmet, the Tunis couchsurfing group and even the university lecturers observed was that the "cosmopolitanism" claimed by many Western people is, in practice, neither egalitarian nor universal. Many Western couchsurfers – so it was often argued – are cosmopolites only while on tour; once they return home, they keep their houses closed to people whom they consider completely different in terms of culture or religion. It is difficult to provide consistent proofs that would substantiate such an argument. What perhaps matters more here is that – whether translating actual realities or not – this argument and the general feeling of rejection it articulates have become part of a wider common sense within the Arab world. A common reaction that I observed among many Tunisian couchsurfers was to refer to Koranic injunctions and other Islamic sources to explain "their" openness to foreigners (Buchberger, Chapter 4). In the eyes of my interlocutors, this openness is somehow distinguished from the "open-mindedness" claimed to be espoused by many Western cosmopolites, which the respondents frequently considered to be merely a specific fashion or lifestyle among Western middle classes rather than a "genuine" interest in others. In this sense, the quest for the "real", which – we argue – underpins Western alternative tourism movements and also much of the impetus of the couchsurfing community, is here pushed even further.

The frictions occurring in the context of couchsurfing encounters in Tunisia thus speak to the ways in which some local surfers feel socially excluded in a wider sense from the dominant cosmopolitan narrative among Western members. In a national context in which the Tunisian government had long institutionalised a narrative of Tunisia built upon its presumed European ancestry, this exclusion becomes even more "painful". In their encounters with their presumed Western "relatives", the expectation of reaffirming a shared kinship between Tunisian and European couchsurfers is denied. Instead, the Tunisians experience that the travels of their Western guests are to a large extent driven by Orientalist images that reaffirm the Maghreb and its inhabitants as radically different.

It appears that it is first and foremost this exclusion that leads to the emancipation of other, alternative cosmopolitanisms. The phenomenon is not new, as Edward Said (1994 [1979]) stresses in his work on the historical constitution of the "Orient" built by, and in opposition to, the West. The Orient had to compensate for the shortcomings of the modernist project and provide what was considered to be missing in the modern world. In a context of perceived or real rejection, it seems the natural thing to do to generate new forms of "vernacular" cosmopolitanism (Werbner, 2008) by mobilising religion, gender or whatever other criteria are used to define belonging (cf. Forte, 2010) as overarching reference points. The paradox and sad irony of the contra-cosmopolitanism generated among the mostly educated middle-class members of the couchsurfing community in Tunisia is that the political rhetoric of the "clash of civilizations" noted by Samuel Huntington – which arguably has incited much of the anti-Islamic resentments in Western countries since the mid-1990s – is also used in the Arab world, to foster limits and polarise boundaries between Self and Other.

The lively discussion at the Tunis couchsurfing meeting introduced another element. Many, if not most couchsurfers said that they had a more immediate understanding of, and felt more at ease with, Muslim guests. Similarly, a frequent argument brought forward at the couchsurfing community forum "Muslim couchsurfers" is that a shared "Muslim" ethics of hospitality more easily creates feelings of closeness and familiarity among couchsurfers. This latter observation points to another dimension of couchsurfing experience and culture which goes beyond the rhetoric of cosmopolitan discourse or feelings of belonging or rejection – something that can be anthropologically analysed in terms of different "regimes of hospitality" that emerge in the field of contact with strangers.

Regimes of hospitality and the power to dramatise one's guest's experiences

Like all forms of hospitality and most forms of human relation, couchsurfing implies expectations of reciprocity that are framed within the specific cultures of hosts and guests. Dennis Zuev, in his study on couchsurfing hospitality in Siberia (Chapter 3), argues that the hosting of guests is socially regulated by what he calls "regimes of hospitality". He explains that couchsurfing generates a cosmopolitan realm mainly for the guests and travellers, yet remains governed by localised hospitality norms and cultures for the hosts. While guests are often candidly invited to "feel at home", they are not free to act as they please. Instead, he explains – through his own, self-reflexive account as a host in his Siberian home town – they are assigned specific locales within the private home, they are expected to visit – and enjoy – specific sites proposed by the host, and they are also expected to behave in specific ways. There are always rules and boundaries to behaviour which hosts and guests are woven into, often unconsciously (Durkheim, 1964[1938]).

Zuev gives an account of hosting the Italian Argentinean couchsurfer Marco to illustrate his frequent disappointments about the ways in which his (mainly Western) guests acted. Marco promised to cook "real" Italian pasta. Zuev could not see the point or particularity of eating pasta, which had become an ordinary dish in his town. But he accepted the gesture of Marco, who wanted to offer something in exchange for the hospitality he had received. Zuev bought ingredients to prepare the pasta and, the night before his guest's departure, reminded him about his promise. Marco no longer wanted to cook pasta, and Zuev was not happy – not because of not being able to enjoy Italian pasta, but because of the breach of promise. In his account, Zuev explains that in his Siberian home town, hospitality used to be primarily about offering shelter to strangers – hunters, traders and run-away prisoners. A new type of stranger appeared at the end of the Cold War in the 1990s in the form of (again, mainly Western) backpackers travelling along the Tran-Siberian railway to China. For this new type of stranger, making a journey through an "odd" land had in itself become the main attraction. Zuev explains that he realised Marco's, and his subsequent Western guests', predispositions towards Siberia, and decided to show them an alternative, valuable and "true" image. He took Marco on a long hiking trip through his favourite landscapes. Marco became exhausted halfway through the hike, seemingly not appreciating the landscape that Zuev loved so much. He eventually left early. Disappointed by the experience, Zuev wrote him a positive – but not an "extremely" positive – review. Marco and his subsequent guests were just "normal" couchsurfers and did not produce any specific "emotional kick". At the same time, Zuev describes how he felt like a "hero" when taking charge of his guests, becoming the conductor of the spectacle put up for them, producer of awe-inspiring landscapes, gatekeeper of intimate knowledge about local life and narrator of personalised stories and interpretations about a specific local reality.

In one of the first sociological essays on hospitality, Georg Simmel (1950) discusses how the ambivalent unity of nearness and remoteness involved in human relations is organised in the specific phenomenon of the stranger. The latter, he explains, is able to challenge notions of strangeness and possibilities of commonality among hosts and guests, and can thus either accentuate or dissipate conceptions of Self and Other. According to Hocart (2004 [1952]), in various historical contexts – such as ancient Greece, India and Fiji – strangers were seen as potentially divine messengers or returning ancestors. Because they usually belong to an "extra-ordinary" world, they were, in the belief of their hosts, "suitable vehicle[s] for the apparition of the Gods" (Pitt-Rivers, 1977:101). In a similar vein, the stoic philosopher Seneca, in his *Letters to Lucilius*, proposed disregarding the social status of a stranger, who could as well be a knight, slave or beggar, and solemnly consider their soul, which may be "god dwelling as a guest in a human body" (Seneca, 65AD:Let. 31/11). To respond to the ambiguity of foreigners, gods and ghosts, most human societies have developed practices of hospitality that allow them to "exercise power"[4] over these strangers and deal with their potentially harmful qualities or intentions (Graburn, 2012). Julian Pitt-Rivers (1977) defines the social logic of hospitality in terms of a double strategy aimed at both socialising and containing strangers by transforming them into guests. In his *The People of the Sierra* (1954), Pitt-Rivers explains that from the perspective of a community of villagers, anthropologists and other strangers who walk into a village behave like children, ignoring, and therefore breaking, rules, and having to be socialised. At the same time, the relative magic often associated with such strangers can help to empower the host, in particular where these strangers pertain to the mythical world of powerful foreign enemies, spirits, divinities or ancestors (Sahlins, 1995). For Claude Lévi-Strauss (1974), the symbolic and sometimes material consumption of stranger-enemies and also of dead family relatives is a method to nullify ontological Otherness (and thus to neutralise the danger of contagion this Otherness implies), and at the same time to appropriate the power of the Other in the Self.

Yet, Lévi-Strauss' metaphor of cannibalistic consumption only provides a partial explanation. Hocart (2004) stresses that within a system of anticipated reciprocity, instead of being eaten, strangers are actually more often treated with due respect; in return (because there is an expected return), the host expects favours either immediately, or in later life from God or any other transcendental entity. The ontological difference between host

4 | The word "hospitality" is likely to stem from a combination of the Latin noun *hostis* (itself derived from the proto-Indo-European *g'óstis*, meaning stranger, enemy, ghost, guest) and the Latin verb *petere* (attack, engage, exercise power over). From the contraction of the two terms are derived the noun *hospitero* (literally: the [one] "exercising power over a stranger"; practically used as "lord of strangers" or "the host") and the verb *hospitor* (in practical usage,"to *be* a guest"; cf. Lewis & Short, 1879). (Cf. also Candeia & da Col, 2012 who refer to Derrida, 2000, who in turn refers to Benveniste, 1969).

and guest is here not neutralised, but kept alive and nurtured – like the Olympic flame or the bone relics of saints that are believed to maintain an "authentic link" (Steward, 1984) to their mythical origins. In this way, the ontological work of hospitality is to operate a dialectic process through which Self and Other (which in mythical time belonged to a wider whole) are separated and brought back into contact, only to be separated once again. The prerequisite condition of hospitality is the delineation of Other estranged of Self, yet possibly also as part of Self in a hidden or uncanny way (Kristeva, 1991). From this point of view, hospitality reveals itself to be a powerful social institution to maintain and renew social and cosmic order. Its study may embrace any form of practice by means of which a priori strangers and strange worlds (which may equally be people, spirits and material cultures or abstract models, techniques and knowledge) are accommodated and encompassed. A series of great examples are provided in a recent special issue of the *Journal of the Royal Anthropological Institute* edited by Candea and da Col (2012).

Dennis Zuev's account illustrates how the materiality of travellers from Europe and North America arriving in Siberia brings to life a locally held imaginary of the "Western world". The hospitality towards these travellers enables local hosts to engage and appropriate the "magic" associated with this foreign world, and to integrate a part of it into the social intimacy of their home. The home itself is transformed as a result of this contact and contamination. It becomes a locale that reaches out beyond the immediate contexts of the here and now and opens up possibilities for associations with a wider world beyond – not unlike religious shrines functioning as connectors to the worlds of the divine in other contexts. The hospitality towards couchsurfing strangers – similar to the hospitality towards saints and spirits – allows the host to emancipate, within a micro-local context, an identity based upon relations within a wider cosmos. It transforms living rooms into ceremonial grounds celebrating the world citizenship of their owners. Yet, Zuev explains, the magic can fade. Where foreign travellers provide no more "emotional kick", where they become easily predictable "Lonely-planetized" tourists, they and the worlds they represent lose much of their appeal. In such cases, the power relations are inverted. The stranger is no longer imbued with uncertain, magical or potentially dangerous powers that need to be contained or socialised. Instead, the stranger is lost in translation, and is easily manipulated by the host. Zuev observes that for the host, to exercise power over the guest by "conducting" his or her experiences can be a playful pleasure in itself.

What Zuev's account also illustrates is that couchsurfing develops a form of touristic hospitality at a hitherto little-accustomed scale. Most forms of traditional mass-produced tourism are based on industry- or state-orchestrated regimes of tourism hospitality, carefully planned through tourism development and marketing strategies. Through the production of signage, maps and interpretation sites, the touristic strangers are (usually) successfully contained in specific spaces and itineraries within the urban or natural landscape. The strategic renovations and architectural re-developments of the urban centres of most European capitals during the 19th and 20th centuries here provide prime examples. They became strategically produced miniatures to showcase what the specific nations wanted to be and be about. Addressing both domestic and international tourists, the rebuilt city centres of Paris, London, Berlin or Lisbon ostentatiously displayed – and touristically ceremonialised – the presumed wealth of their respective colonial empires, the genius of their respective technological, artistic and architectural progress, the stories and references of their respective imagined national cultural ancestries and their dominant values or "personalities".

In the context of couchsurfing, hospitality practice is performed essentially at the scale of the private domestic home. The logic and the means of accommodating strangers at that scale seem to remain largely similar to those of publicly performed hospitality. Karen Halttunen (1989), for instance, observes how the traditional parlour in the front of the house of many Western households (initially used only during the mourning of the dead) has evolved into a specifically reserved space for the accommodation of and catering to strangers and guests. She argues that, with the emergence of the "transparent" person as a societal ideal in the USA in the early 20th century, the hidden back regions and secret gardens of the house (and the person) disappeared, making the living room a "transparent" symbolic, social and logistic centre of social life. In practice, the ideal described by Halttunen was not achieved; even if reduced to a more private scale, back regions, in the form of sleeping rooms, garden huts or hobby cellars continue to exist. At the same time the living room becomes a place to socialise with different types of a priori foreigners: guests, strangers, new-born babies, saints, spirits and "souvenir-relics" from the last holiday. The structure and function of hospitality observed in these cases remain similar to the hospitality of state-orchestrated public spaces or formerly religious ones to engage the supernatural and devine. The phenomenon of hospitality thus seems able to transform and reappear at different scales of social life (cf. Candea and da Col (2012), who refer to Michael Herzfeld's (1987) work on Mediterranean hospitality). In the context of couchsurfing, it usually evolves within spaces governed by families and local cultural norms. Bernard Schéou (Chapter 6) argues that the hospitality towards foreign couchsurfers in Vietnam evolves in the field of tension between social aspirations to participate in a "modern", global world and the largely resilient norms of Confucian hospitality which prevent the accommodation of strangers in the domestic house. To deal with this tension, the a priori "guests" are commonly treated as, and transformed into, "friends" or pseudo-kin, which allows them to be welcomed and integrated into the family home. In other cases, couchsurfing hosts hide their activity from their wider families, conscious about breaking cultural taboos.

As demonstrated by Dennis Zuev's story, hosting foreigners at home eventually can become a transformative experience for the hosts themselves, allowing them to realise their own cultural difference as much as that of their guests. Zuev explains that he had to learn to deal with his guests, to anticipate their expectations and deal with the disappointments when guests did not act as expected. In the end, he realised that he did not provide access to any form of "real", Siberia, but had become the producer of a specific Siberian fantasy world that he loved, and hoped his guests would love as well.

Couchsurfing in Brisbane (David Picard)

While Couchsurfing.org is to a large extent about facilitating one-to-one contact between hosts and guests, it also provides its members with an online-to-offline community platform used to create interest groups, organise events, meet up and form friendships at the local scale. In the next and final section, David Picard will draw on his experience of couchsurfing at Gustavo's in Australia to explore this community aspect.

Gustavo was waiting in his car outside Brisbane airport. It was three in the morning, raining and steaming hot. My girlfriend and I had just arrived from a 32-hour journey from Lisbon, with stopovers in Madrid, Dubai and Singapore. We were tired from the trip, and also excited to finally be in Australia. We had found Gustavo's profile page on the top of the list of the Brisbane couchsurfers, and sent him a short message requesting if we could stay at his place for a couple of days. He had agreed to our request and offered to pick us up at the airport.

When driving into town, we spoke in Portuguese and later changed to English. Gustavo was in his early thirties, a son of South-American immigrants, and had grown up on Australia's west coast. He had come to Brisbane to work as a contractor for a mining company. We arrived at his home, an executive-style two-bedroom flat on the top floor of a newly built complex in the centre of Brisbane's West End. The flat was sparsely decorated; most of the stuff had been put there by the property agent. Gustavo showed us "our" room, a large double bedroom with en suite bathroom, left us the house keys and went to bed. When we woke up the next day, he had left for work. We had breakfast at a coffee place outside the building. Upon our return, he was back in the flat and suggested a programme of things we could do together. We took his car to drive to a forest site just outside town, and walked up a hill with a grand panoramic view over the city. Gustavo told us about his family, who had stayed on the west coast, and his involvement in the local couchsurfing community, through which he had met most of his friends. We later went to a restaurant, had some drinks and met some of his friends in a dancing place. We were dead tired and returned to the house early to go to sleep. He had planned another programme for us for the following day – going to a local coffee house, visiting the South Bank area, going to an Afro music concert and a Latin dance night. We eventually politely declined and stayed on our own.

After moving to Lisbon, I had continued to participate in the couchsurfing community and hosted a couple of people at my flat. I also attended a dinner organised by the Lisbon group. The meeting of people who were mostly strangers to each other at first created a peculiar ambiance. Yet, the experience of sitting down together at tables, sharing a meal and later going out for drinks dissipated many of the initial tensions. I made some tentative contacts, most of whom I never met again. Some others eventually became friends to go out and hang out with. Through a friend of a couchsurfing friend, I also met my girlfriend, who joined me on my trip to Brisbane. There, we found a house-sit through the website Sabbaticalhomes.org, which was to become available a couple of days after our arrival. Until then, we stayed at Gustavo's. Throughout our stay in Queensland, we used the couchsurfing website to meet people at picnics in the park, attend a weekend party in the private house of a Mexican-Australian couple and go on a camping trip with a French couple. Through the repetition of meetings, relations with some people became stronger; in any case, it created familiarity and a sense of community belonging. Only a few of the couchsurfing members who were part of our Brisbane friends were actually couchsurfing at that time; most were somehow displaced, and used the website to meet people and make new friendships. In the actual meetings of couchsurfers, the criterion of nationality frequently moved to the background and the shared experience of meeting people and doing things together – the emotions of transhumance that Paula Bialski (2007) talks about, or maybe more simply the emotions of feeling part of a community – came to the fore. Surfing, which initially defined the moment of riding a wave with the help of a surfboard or pirogue, seemed an appropriate metaphor to describe these emotions. Like the happiness that overcomes a surfer riding waves in the sea, these emotions were mostly ephemeral. We met many people whom we would otherwise have considered somehow "odd" in terms of their profession, lifestyle or personality – at the very least, people who, through our established social practices and friendship networks, we would have had very little chance to meet. As Dennis Zuev argues, it was certainly more interesting for us to surf a couch and to discover the exoticisms of the ordinary life-worlds of others than to host surfers who will always "just" be surfers.

It is of course a candid surfer-centric claim that couchsurfing – the "riding" of other people's private homes and domestic intimacies – is making a "better" world. The chapters of this book show that couchsurfing is not accessible to everyone, and that its specific culture of "openness" often hides a resilient set of stereotypes which may be deeply alien and even offensive to many people. Paradoxically, in a world in which communication technologies, mobility and migration have challenged many established narratives about national, local, ethnic, religious or cultural belonging, tourism practices like couchsurfing, and the cosmopolitan ideals they mediate, rhetorically often reconfirm and reinforce such narratives. Following Theodor Lessing's (1919) observations, made a hundred years ago, the modern idea of history and the allegory of a timeless Eden as its anchor point continue to supply a widely hegemonic, global framework to make sense of time, becoming and being in the world. According to Jean Baudrillard (1998), notions like culture, religion or nation are here no longer necessarily signs of difference, but of social differentiation within a common social space. As

De-Jung Chen shows in her chapter on Taiwan (Chapter 5), learning about this framework of differentiations and the cultural stereotypes it projects upon Self and Others becomes a means to participate in the cosmopolitan world system.

At the same time, while cosmopolitanism is often so easily deconstructed and pushed aside as a merely aesthetic garment of unbalanced global power relations, it actually proposes a pragmatic way to live together and to organise human life at the global scale. In our view, it is the preserve of the spheres of political debate and activism, not academia, to debate or judge its moral goodness – or what Peggy Swain (2009) has called the "cosmopolitan hope" of tourism. However, as social activists and as couchsurfing tourists – and not acting under the cover of a putatively ideologically neutral academia – we can state that Couchsurfing has certainly helped us to make *our* world "better", to cultivate our obsession with the search for divine beauty that we know we will not find, to meet like-minded and like-mindedly odd people, many of whom continue to live in our memories. It has helped us to candidly cultivate our garden, and given birth to a beautiful little barracuda =).

References

Adler, J. (1989) "Origins of sightseeing". *Annals of Tourism Research* 16:7-29.

Amit, V. and Rapport, N. (2012) *Community, cosmopolitanism and the problem of human commonality*. London: Pluto.

Appiah, K.A. (2006) *Cosmopolitanism: ethics in a world of strangers*. New York: W.W. Norton & Co.

Baudrillard, J. (1998) *The consumer society: myths and structures*. London: Sage.

Beck, U. (2006) *The cosmopolitan vision*. Cambridge and Malden: Polity.

Benveniste, E. (1969) *Le vocabulaire des institutions indoeuropeennes: sommaires, tableau et index etablis*. Paris: Editions de minuit.

Bialski, P. (2007) *Intimate tourism: friendships in a state of mobility – the case of the online hospitality network*. Warsaw: University of Warsaw.

Bialski, P. (2012) *Becoming intimately mobile*. Vol. 2. Warsaw Studies in Culture and Society. Frankfurt: Peter Lang.

Binnie, J., et al. (2006) "Grounding cosmopolitan urbanism: approaches, practices and policies". In J. Binnie et al. (eds.) *Cosmopolitan urbanism.* London: Routledge, pp.1-34.

Bruner, E.M. (2005) *Culture on tour: ethnographies of travel.* Chicago: University of Chicago Press.

Butcher, J. (2003) *The moralisation of tourism: sun, sand ... and saving the world?* London: Routledge.

Candea, M. and Da Col, G. (2012) "The return to hospitality". *Journal of the Royal Anthropological Institute* 18, Issue Supplement S1:1-19.

Cohen, E. (2004) *Contemporary tourism: diversity and change.* Amsterdam: Elsevier.

Couchsurfing.org (2012) https://www.couchsurfing.org (accessed 7 October 2012).

Crossley, É. (2012) "Affect and moral transformation in young volunteer tourists". In D. Picard and M. Robinson (eds.) *Emotion in motion: tourism, affect and transformation.* Farnham: Ashgate, pp.85-98.

Derrida, J. (2000) *Of hospitality: Anne Dufourmantelle invites Jacques Derrida to respond.* Translated by R. Bowlby. Stanford: Stanford University Press.

Diep, M., Drabble, S. and Young, C. (2006) "Living with difference? The 'cosmopolitan city' and urban reimaging in Manchester, UK". *Urban Studies* 43:1687-1714.

Donald, S.H., Kevin, C. and Kofman, E. (eds.) (2009) *Branding cities: cosmopolitanism, parochialism, and social change.* Abingdon: Routledge.

Dowdeswell, T. (2011) "Cosmopolitanism, custom, and complexity: Kant's cosmopolitan norms in action". *Cosmopolitan Civil Societies: An Interdisciplinary Journal* 3(3):176-196.

Dower, N. (2003) *An introduction to global citizenship.* Edinburgh: Edinburgh University Press.

Durkheim, E. (1964 [1938]) *The rules of sociological method.* New York: Free Press of Glencoe.

Feifer, M. (1985) "The imperial Roman". In M. Feifer (ed.) *Going places. The ways of the tourist from imperial Rome to the present day.* London: MacMillan, pp. 7-26.

Forte, M.C. (ed.) (2010) *Indigenous cosmopolitans: transnational and transcultural indigeneity in the twenty-first century.* New York: Peter Lang.

Frankland, S. (2009) "The bulimic consumption of pygmies: regurgitating an image of otherness". In M. Robinson and D. Picard (eds.) *The framed world: tourism, tourists and photography*. Farnham: Ashgate, pp. 95-115.

Friese, H. (2009) "The limits of hospitality". *Paragraph* 32(1): 51-68.

Germann Molz, J. (2011) "Cosmopolitanism and consumption". In M. Rovisco and M. Nowicka (eds.) *The Ashgate research companion to cosmopolitanism*. Farnham: Ashgate, pp. 33-52.

Germann Molz, J. (2011) "CouchSurfing and network hospitality: 'It's not just about the furniture'". *Hospitality & Society* 1(3): 215-225.

Graburn, N.H.H. (1983) *To pray, pay and play: the cultural structure of Japanese domestic tourism*. Aix-en-Provence: Centre des hautes études touristiques.

Graburn, N.H.H. (2012) "Hospitality, a human universal: gift or commodity?" *Journal of Guangxi University for Nationalities* (Philosophy and Social Sciences Edition) 5: 10-15.

Greenblatt, S. (1980) *Renaissance self-fashioning: from More to Shakespeare*. Chicago: University of Chicago Press.

Halttunen, K. (1989) "From parlor to living room: domestic space and the culture of personality". In S.J. Bronner (ed.) *Consuming visions: accumulation and display of goods in America, 1880-1920*. New York: Norton.

Heal, F. (1990) *Hospitality in early modern England*. Oxford: Clarendon Press.

Herzfeld, M. (1987) "'As in your own house': hospitality, ethnography, and the stereotype of Mediterranean society". In David D. Gilmore (ed.) *Honor and shame and the unity of the Mediterranean*. Washington, D.C.: American Anthropological Association, pp. 75-89.

Hine, C. (2000) *Virtual ethnography*. London: Thousand Oaks.

Hocart, A.M. (2004 [1952]) *The life-giving myth*. London: Routledge.

Huntington, S.P. (1996) *The clash of civilizations and the remaking of world order*. New York: Simon & Schuster.

Kant, I. (1903 [1795]) *Perpetual peace: a philosophical essay*, with a preface by R. Latta. Translated by Campbell Smith. London: Allen & Unwin.

Kristeva, J. (1991) *Strangers to ourselves*. New York: Columbia University Press.

Lewis. C T. and Short, C. (1879) *A Latin Dictionary*, Oxford: Clarendon Press.

Lanfant, M.-F. and Graburn, N.H.H. (1992) "International tourism reconsidered: the principle of the alternative". In V.L. Smith and W.R. Eadington (eds.) *Tourism alternatives: potentials and problems in the development of tourism.* Chichester: John Wiley, pp.88-112.

Lashley, C. and Morrison, A.J. (eds.) (2001) *In search of hospitality: theoretical perspectives and debates.* Oxford: Butterworth-Heinemann.

Lashley, C., Lynch, P. and Morrison, A.J. (eds.) (2007) *Hospitality: a social lens.* Amsterdam: Elsevier.

Laxson, J.D. (1991) "*How 'we' see 'them': tourism and Native Americans*". *Annals of Tourism Research* 18(3): 365-91.

Lenz, R. (2010) "'Hotel Royal' and other spaces of hospitality: tourists and migrants in the Mediterranean". In T. Selwyn and J. Scott (eds.) *Thinking through tourism.* New York: Berg Publishers, pp.209-230.

Lessing, T. (1919) *Geschichte als Sinngebung des Sinnlosen.* München: Beck.

Levi-Strauss, C. (1974) *Tristes tropiques.* New York: Atheneum.

Löfgren, O. (2002) *On holiday: a history of vacationing.* Berkeley, CA: University of California Press.

MacCannell, D. (1976) *The tourist: a new theory of the leisure class.* New York: Schocken.

Okely, J. (1996) *Own or other culture.* London: Routledge.

Picard, D. and Robinson, M. (eds.) (2012) *Emotion in motion: tourism, affect and tranformation.* London: Ashgate.

Picard, D. (2010) "'Being a model for the world': performing Creoleness in La Réunion". *Social Anthropology* 18:302-315.

Picard, D. (2011) *Tourism, magic and modernity: cultivating the human garden.* Oxford: Berghahn.

Pitt-Rivers, J. (1954) *The people of the Sierra.* London: Weidenfeld & Nicolson.

Pitt-Rivers, J. (1977) *The fate of Shechem, or the politics of sex: essays in the anthropology of the Mediterranean.* Cambridge: Cambridge University Press.

Powdermaker, H. (1966) *Stranger and friend: the way of an anthropologist.* New York: W.W. Norton.

Rapport, N. (2012) *Anyone: the cosmopolitan subject of anthropology.* New York: Berghahn.

Régi, T. (2012) "Tourism, leisure and work in an East African pastoral society". *Anthropology Today* 28(5):3-7.

Rosello, M. (2001) *Postcolonial hospitality: the immigrant as guest.* Stanford: Stanford University Press.

Sahlins, M. (1993) "Goodbye to tristes tropiques: ethnography in the context of modern world history". *Journal of Modern History* 65:1-25.

Said, E.W. (1994 [1979]) *Orientalism*. Harmondsworth: Penguin.

Salazar, N.B. (2010) "Tourism and cosmopolitanism: a view from below". *International Journal of Tourism Anthropology* 1(1):55-69.

Selwyn, T. (1996) *The tourist image: myths and myth making in tourism*. Chichester: John Wiley.

Seneca (65 A.D.) "Letter 31. On siren songs". In his *Moral letters to Lucilius*. http://en.wikisource.org/wiki/Moral_letters_to_Lucilius/Letter_31 (accessed 28 Nov 2012).

Simmel, G. (1950) *The sociology of Georg Simmel*. Translated by Kurt H. Wolff. Glencoe, IL: Free Press.

Steward, S. (1984) *On longing: narratives of the miniature, the gigantic, the souvenir, the collection*. Baltimore: Johns Hopkins University Press.

Still, J. (2010) *Derrida and hospitality: theory and practice*. Edinburgh: Edinburgh University Press.

Swain, M.B. (2001) "*Cosmopolitan* tourism and minority politics in the Stone Forest". In T.C. Beng, S. Cheung and Y. Hui (eds.) *Tourism, anthropology and Chinese society*. Bangkok: White Press.

Swain, M.B. (2009) "The cosmopolitan hope of tourism: critical action and worldmaking vistas". *Tourism Geographies* 11(4):505-525.

Urry, J. (2002) *The tourist gaze*. London: Sage Publications.

Wang, N. (2000). *Tourism and modernity: sociological analysis*. Amsterdam: Pergamon.

Werbner, P. (2008) "Introduction: towards a new cosmopolitan anthropology". In P. Werbner (ed.) *Anthropology and the new cosmopolitanism: rooted, feminist and vernacular perspectives*. Oxford: Berg, pp. 1-29.

2. Cosmopolitans on the Couch: Mobile Hospitality and the Internet

Jennie Germann Molz

On 1 May 2001, Ramon Stoppelenburg left his home in Zwolle in the Netherlands to travel around the world for a few years.[1] In many ways, the 24-year-old Dutch student was like thousands of other university students around Europe who take a year off to travel the world, usually on a shoestring budget. But, unlike other travellers, Ramon embarked on his trip without *any* money. In fact, Ramon planned to circumnavigate the globe on less than a shoestring: he planned to do it for free, by hitchhiking and by staying with the hundreds of hosts who had invited him via his website LetMeStayForADay.com. Months before his departure date, Ramon had launched the website to allow people from around the world to submit invitations to host Ramon for a night. The "deal", according to Ramon, was that in exchange for giving him a place to sleep for the night, a meal and Internet access, hosts would find their towns, their homes and possibly their cooking skills documented in the daily reports Ramon posted on his increasingly popular website.

According to newspaper coverage of the site, Ramon had become the world's most famous homeless guy – a Dutch freeloader for whom "going Dutch" meant not paying at all. Ramon's website chronicled his ongoing journey in minute detail, allowing an ever-growing audience to follow him virtually as he travelled physically to the homes of over 500 hosts in a dozen countries over a two-year period. The discussion forum he hosted

---

1 | This chapter was originally published in *Mobilizing hospitality: the ethics of social relations in a mobile world*, ed. by J. Germann Molz and S. Gibson (Ashgate, 2007). Funding was provided for this research through an Economic and Social Research Council Postdoctoral Fellowship (Award PTA-026-27-0623).

on the website also became an active hub where people could interact with Ramon and with each other. Here, past hosts and friends vouched for Ramon's charm and sincerity, future hosts expressed their eagerness to meet him, and strangers from around the world debated, criticised and praised Ramon's project and his performance as a perpetual guest.

In addition to Ramon's LetMeStayForADay.com project, an increasing number of hospitality organisations have appeared online to help travellers find a place to crash for a night or two. This chapter discusses several of these sites, including the HospitalityClub.org, Hospitality Exchange at hospex.net, Servas International, GlobalFreeloaders.com and Couchsurfing.org. These websites operate primarily as "members only" communities that employ databases of thousands of members to connect hosts and guests online and face-to-face. Members can search the databases of the websites to look for a host in a particular destination, use profiles to see whether what the host has to offer matches what the traveller needs, submit to various security measures intended to maximise the safety of these encounters between strangers and participate in active-member discussion boards. Though a few of these sites charge a small membership fee, they are all not-for-profit organisations guided largely by the belief that world travel, interpersonal interactions between people from diverse cultures and the generosity of hospitality can spread tolerance, friendship and world peace at a grassroots level. These sites raise several challenging questions about hospitality as a social relation between strangers, about the links between mobility, hospitality and the Internet, and about the way a "global community" is forged, idealised and bounded through the prism of hospitality. In addition to coordinating the logistics of hospitality, these websites act as discursive sites where the moral, ethical and practical aspects of hospitality are contested and controlled.

In this chapter, I discuss several ways in which the Internet, both as a communication medium between geographically dispersed strangers and as a technological fantasy, is used to maintain the propriety of the hospitality relationship, manage the anxieties inherent in moments of hospitality and police the boundaries of the hospitable traveller-host community. First, I examine the way hospitality is understood as a *reciprocal* arrangement between hosts and guests. Like Kant, whose notions of hospitality Derrida explicitly critiques, these hospitality websites emphasise hospitality as a reciprocal exchange. Setting aside for the moment Derrida's critique of contractual formulations of hospitality (a critique I will return to later), I look at how these websites try to maintain the equilibrium of give-and-take in the hospitable encounter. Second, I consider how the *reputation* systems on these websites act as a kind of surveillance mechanism that monitors this reciprocity between hosts and guests, but which also secure the face-to-face meeting between strangers and control the boundaries of the hospitality community. In both of these discussions, we can see how these websites also work to arrange the internal paradoxes that characterise definitions of hospitality. Drawing on Benveniste's (1973) etymology of the term "hospitality", Derrida (2000) highlights its several contradictory meanings, such as "host" *and* "guest", "guest" *and* "parasite", "guest" *and* "enemy". Such indeterminacies give rise to certain anxieties surrounding hospitality, namely the risk that the guest may actually become a parasite or an enemy – a risk that the websites manage through reciprocity and reputation. Finally, I address the paradox of "global community" as it is produced and performed in these hospitality communities. Here, I consider the way a cosmopolitan disposition of open-ness toward difference actually serves to delimit a bounded community of "like-minded" but diverse individuals.

Reciprocity

The hospitality websites in this study govern interactions between strangers within an economy of hospitality that is negotiated in terms of *reciprocity*. In his analysis of the root terms of hospitality – *hospes, hostis* and *potis* – Benveniste argues that hospitality essentially denotes a reciprocal exchange. According to Benveniste, the root *hostis* appeared in various Latin phrases expressing a sense of reciprocity: "repay a kindness", "I promise you a reciprocal service, as you deserve" and "compensation of a benefit", with related terms referring to measurement and equalisation (1973:76). Benveniste explains that *hostis* signifies "he [sic] who stands in a compensatory relationship [...] founded on the idea that a man [sic] is bounded to another (*hostis* always involves the notion of reciprocity) by the obligation to compensate a gift or service from which he has benefited" (ibid.:77). In fact, according to such definitions of hospitality, it is precisely this *reciprocal* exchange that binds people in social solidarity. The websites I look at promote hospitality similarly, as a social pact – one that ensures not only the proper relationship between host and guest in the moment of the hospitality encounter itself, but also as a contract that extends a binding moral code across the whole community. However, the symmetry of the hospitality encounter is always fragile. Because there is always the possibility of an excess, a lack, or a slippage between give and take, the threat of imbalance – the prospect that the guest will take advantage of the host's generosity by taking too much or by *only* taking – must be constantly managed. In other words, guests must not be allowed to turn into *freeloaders*, imposing themselves and drawing parasitically on other people's generosity without sharing in the cost or responsibility. For example, Gibson (2003) describes how unwelcome strangers, such as asylum seekers, are often portrayed in the media as parasites who take advantage of the nation's hospitality or welfare system without giving anything back. The websites serve to arbitrate this slippery equation, so it is somewhat confusing to find that in many cases these travellers happily refer to themselves as "freeloaders" on the websites. Much of the media coverage of Ramon's journey refers to him in almost celebratory tones as the "world's biggest freeloader". And one of the websites, GlobalFreeloading.com, uses the word in its title and refers to its members as "freeloaders". Of course, these appropriations of the term "freeloader" are purposefully ironic, foregrounding the anxiety of freeloading while at the same time making it impossible by strictly regulating the reciprocity between hosts and guests. By ironically appropriating terms like "freeloader", these hospitality websites acknowledge the anxieties around parasitism while simultaneously distancing themselves from the highly politicised arena of immigration and "national" hospitality.

Derrida points out that one of the uncertainties of hospitality is "the general problematic of relationships between parasitism and hospitality" (2000:59). He asks: "How can we distinguish between a guest and a parasite?" (ibid.) Each website provides its own parameters for making this distinction, and for ensuring that its members stay on the "guest" side of the divide. For example, when Ramon outlines his "deal" to potential hosts, he makes it clear to his hosts and to his readers that he expects only a place to sleep and a meal, and preferably an Internet connection, so that he can fulfil *his* part of the contract – which is to publish a story about his host on the LetMeStayForADay.com website. For a while, Ramon also incorporated a gift exchange into his project, asking each host to send a little something that he could give to the next host. Eight months into the trip, however, he had to forego the gift exchange when hosts started packing him off with objects that were too bulky or fragile, such as guitars or china teacups.

Elsewhere on his website, Ramon's readers debate the other gestures that need to be factored into the give-take equation. One reader posted: "Hey, I hope you were not only freeloading on others! What did you do in return?" Some of Ramon's critics wondered on the discussion forum whether Ramon said "thank you" often enough to his hosts, or whether he was doing the dishes or helping out enough around the house. Other readers, often past hosts, usually chimed in that Ramon *did* say "thank you" or *did* do the dishes, even if he did not write about it in his report. In these interchanges, the online community policed Ramon's "deal" and ensured that the encounters with his hosts were reciprocated with the proper amount of gratitude and helpfulness, if not monetary compensation.

On other websites, such as Couchsurfing.org and GlobalFreeloaders.com, the social pact of hospitality is itemised in similar terms. For example, in addition to stating what hosts are expected to offer (namely, a place to sleep for the night), Couchsurfing.org clarifies the guest's obligations. The following sample of tips on how to be a "good" couchsurfer highlights the fundamental basis of reciprocity, and hints at some of the anxieties this contract entails:

As a good example of a good Surfer, you do as much as you can to give back to your hosts. This includes doing things like, for example, the dishes or stacking some wood. Maybe you have a special skill that you're willing to share.
Bring a bottle of wine, or a six-pack of beer (go with the micro brew if at all possible, make it at least appear that you are making an effort; since you don't have to pay for a hotel room or hostel, cough up the $ 6-10). The wine is usually a safer bet than beer.
Take a shower even if you took a shower the night before. One of the most important elements of being a good couch surfer is always appearing that you have somewhere to go... if people see you as a drifter with no direction, they will be a little worried about the chance of you trying to camp out on their couch longer than they would like you to.
Nothing is better for a couch surfer than doing the dishes, a role 90 % of the population disdains. Either before you go to sleep, or when you wake up at another person's house first thing in the morning, do the dishes.
Do not put your stuff in the bathroom or take up much space... The more care you take in respecting your host's space, the more your host will appreciate your company and be willing to host another surfer after you're gone.
Always, always send a "Thank-You" postcard from home!

These friendly tips serve to regulate the face-to-face encounters between members in the moment of offering and receiving hospitality. They point to the invisible boundaries between being a visitor or a drifter; between being a good guest or one who overstays their welcome. The specific material and embodied exchanges – hosts providing beds and meals, guests reciprocating with bottles of wine or by keeping themselves tidy and showered – are about the interpersonal relations of giving and receiving hospitality. However, the websites also monitor how individuals give and take as members of the community. For example, the tip on respecting one's host so that they will be willing to host another surfer in the future underlines each traveller's responsibility to positively represent all other travellers in the community.

The very existence of hospitality exchange organisations relies on one basic condition: if you travel as a guest, you must also be willing to be a host. For example, part of Ramon's "deal" was an open invitation to anyone who hosted him to stay at his house once he returned back home to Zwolle. Members of the Hospitality Club, Servas, GlobalFreeloaders and Couchsurfing are expected, and in some cases required, to be both hosts and guests as a condition of their membership in the community. As the GlobalFreeloaders site says: "If there are too many people taking (visitors), and not enough giving (hosting), the system simply won't work".

In order to ensure the proper functioning of the hospitality community as a whole, the websites necessarily blur the distinction between hosts and guests: hosts are just travellers who are not currently on the road, and travellers are hosts who happen to be travelling. As the Hospitality Club website states:

> The idea of The Hospitality Club is to give and to receive help. [...] We don't ask you to do anything. We just offer you the opportunity to meet exactly the people that are going to help you on your next trip and exactly those people that will need your help when they visit your home country.

In this sense, reciprocity imposes a kind of solidarity across the community. All members have been, are currently or soon will be travellers in need of a bed; likewise, all members are expected to be able to offer hospitality at some point. In this way, reciprocity becomes a measure of exclusivity; a way of binding those internal to the community while excluding those who are unable or unwilling to reciprocate properly.

In other ways, the websites naturalise reciprocity as an inevitable attribute of membership in the community. This is done in part by portraying hospitality as *its own* reward. Hosting others is not described as a chore, but rather as a fun way of being a tourist in your own city or living room. As the Couchsurfing.org website tells its members: "By visiting someone you are allowing them to have a vacation even though they are at home". Giving back by hosting is not seen as an obligation, but as a continuation of the pleasures of travel, as the following testimonials from hosts on GlobalFreeloaders.com attest:

Hosting is a great way of meeting people, great conversation, learning new and interesting things from around the globe. Puts excitement into a rather normal day. If you get the chance to host, don't miss it, you'll love it as we have.

We were particularly looking for overseas travellers, so that our children could experience other cultures, languages & food.

I love this site, you appreciate things so much more when you spend time with a traveller... So here I was, with a Canadian girl and a German girl in my home, all at once. I have never had so much fun in my life, all these different cultures mixing at the same time.

I was travelling without a backpack this time!

There are several different ways of thinking through these perceptions of the inherent rewards of hospitality. In one sense, the inherent rewards of hospitality appeal to a cosmopolitan fantasy that infuses all of these websites. The notion of getting close to the Other – so close as to be invited into the stranger's home or to bring the stranger into your own living room – is central to cosmopolitan desires of consuming difference. As these comments suggest, the real thrill of hosting travellers is learning about, interacting with and mixing with different cultures, even without having to pack your suitcase! In another sense, by highlighting these inherent rewards, the websites also mitigate the risk that taking will exceed giving. As long as the "right" kinds of people are included in the community, hosts need not worry that their generosity will be exploited by a freeloading drifter. Instead, they can expect the kind of "reward of cosmopolitanism" expressed in these testimonials. But how do websites ensure that they include the "right" kind of people and put the "right" kinds of difference into circulation within the hospitality community?

One of the key conditions of membership in these communities is the reciprocal exchange of trust. As the Couchsurfing.org website advises its members: "Ask trust in return for your trust". Trust is notoriously difficult to establish in online settings, and regulating trust in contexts of hospitality is especially complex. Thus, a second way that these websites ensure the proper relations of hospitality is by coordinating systems of safety and security within this context of risk.

REPUTATION

Benveniste highlights another indeterminate definition in which *hostis* can be understood: as either "guest" or "enemy". He says that "to explain the connexion between 'guest' and 'enemy' it is usually supposed that both derived their meaning from 'stranger', a sense which is still attested in Latin. The notion 'favourable stranger' developed to 'guest'; that of 'hostile stranger' to 'enemy'" (Benveniste, 1973:75). Hospitality is always a risky affair, fraught with the anxiety that the guest may become a parasite, or worse, the enemy.

As with the ironic deployment of the term "freeloader" on his website, Ramon also raised the fear that the guest may be an enemy with an image that recurs in several places on his website, and that graces the cover of the book he published about his journey. The image is a photograph of Ramon hitchhiking at the side of the road with a hand-painted sign that says "I Don't Kill". Ramon took the risks associated with the stranger to their logical extreme, tapping into the anxieties associated with hospitality in general, and especially hitchhiking. Ramon's sign raises fundamental questions: how can we know whether the stranger will be "favourable" or "hostile"? Whom can we trust, and what constitutes trustworthy information about the strangers we might meet on the road?

Trust is as crucial to the effective functioning of hospitality communities as reciprocity, and the websites seek to circulate trust as a way of ensuring safety in the physical encounters between members. This is done through a variety of security systems that combine online information with physical verification. Among these are systems for verifying members' identities: face-to-face interviews between existing members and potential members and the availability of identity profiles that hosts can match against the traveller who shows up at their door.

The most extensive security system that these websites operate is the "reputation system". Reputation systems, which are common in commercial websites like eBay or Amazon marketplace, are like short-cuts for establishing trust between strangers in online settings. As members have dealings with each other – whether online or in an embodied hospitality encounter – they can provide comments about each other to build up individual members' "reputations". For example, after having a traveller come visit, a host might add to that traveller's profile positive or negative comments about their behaviour as a guest. Similarly, the traveller can post comments about the host. These comments constitute the member's reputation and can be made visible to all other members.[2]

Resnick, Zeckhauser, Friedman and Kuwabara explain how online reputation systems work: "A reputation system collects, distributes and aggregates feedback about participants' past behaviour [...] these systems help people decide whom to trust, encourage trustworthy behaviour, and deter participation by those who are unskilled or dishonest" (2000:45-46). In their study of eBay and similar peer-to-peer retail sites, Resnick et al. attribute the counter-intuitively high rate of successful transactions on eBay to the use of reputation systems and the ability of these systems to foster trust in the absence of other factors. Without face-to-face interactions, known histories, the prospect of future interactions and social consequences for good or bad behaviour, reputation systems lend "the shadow of the future

2 | As Derrida (2000) reminds us, all gestures of hospitality must necessarily entail some risk. It is striking that these websites negotiate risk by invoking the notion of "security" in terms of trust and reputation precisely at a time when debates around national security are dominated by sentiments of suspicion and disbelief. It is important to note, therefore, that discourses of domestic hospitality (as evidenced in these websites) are intricately related to the discourses and policies of national security that proliferated following the terrorist attacks of 11 September 2001. For one thing, the terrorist attacks in New York had repercussions for Ramon's project, as several of the New York residents who had signed up online to host him were, for various reasons, unable to fulfil their offers after the terrorist attacks. More generally, offers to host the traveller in one's home are contingent on the nation first welcoming the traveller across its borders, a welcome that is increasingly regulated.

to each transaction by creating an expectation that other people will look back on it" (ibid.:46). Reputation systems establish histories for members and make these accounts of past actions visible to all other members. Future interactions can then be established based on these reports of past behaviour. This form of interpersonal surveillance within the online community disciplines members' behaviour both online and offline, ensuring that individuals act properly as hosts or guests, and punishing them when they do not.

The discourse surrounding the reputation systems on the hospitality websites intimates that they are in place more to ensure the physical safety of their members than as means to complain that a guest left the bathroom a mess or that a host only offered white wine at dinner. One of the most common themes on each website's "Frequently Asked Questions" page is safety: is it safe to go stay with a stranger or invite one to crash on your couch? The Couchsurfing.org website operates interrelated forms of reputation systems that act as gatekeepers to the core, and presumably "safe", group of members. First, the site uses a system of "References" and "Friend Links". Anyone can leave a reference for any other couchsurfer, building up each member's reputation. Friend Links allow travellers to associate themselves with other reputable travellers. As the website explains:

> Every user is linked to the other users he/she knows in the system through a network of References and Friend Links. These features help other users determine how trustworthy you are, based on the quantity and "quality" of the people you know and also if you've been vouched for.

Second, Couchsurfing.org employs a system of "vouching" that safeguards access to the "core" network of friends:

> **Here's how it works!**
> Vouching on Couchsurfing.com is a security system. It signifies an elevated level of trust for those members who have become vouched for. To become vouched for, someone who is already vouched for must vouch for you...
>
> **Core Network**
> You can only be vouched for if you are connected to the original "core" network of couch surfing members. It is that "core" network of friends (connected through friend links) that is the vouched for network. How do you become vouched for if

you are not part of that network? Easy. Go and surf with someone who is vouched for. After they meet you and get to know you, they can vouch for you.

Finally, for a fee of $ 25, members can also get "verified". The verification process is an identity check that substantiates the name and address that the individual provides. The reputation systems and other security systems that these hospitality websites put into place have two related effects. First, they bind the community even closer together as a "safe" environment in which members are responsible for keeping the community safe. Resnick et al. note that "as a solution to the ubiquitous problem of trust in new short-term relationships on the Internet, reputation systems have immediate appeal; the participants themselves create a safe community" (2000:48). For example, members of the Hospitality Club are encouraged to report on each other for the safety of all:

Members leave comments about each other on their "profiles". There you will be able to read the comments of other members about this member and see his/her past guests and hosts, as well as people that trust him/her. Please do write comments about other members yourself – this feature adds security for all of us.

Reputation systems are described through this rhetoric of safety of the community, but their secondary effect is to produce the community as an exclusive site of belonging. These security systems reproduce hospitality as an inherently risky affair but, rather than embracing that riskiness, as Derrida advocates in his writings on hospitality, these websites work to mitigate and contain it, which results in a closed and exclusive community. These reputation systems work to keep the hospitality community openly closed, leaving us with a paradox that I want to discuss in the next section.

The Paradox of Global Community

By using the Internet to administer systems of reciprocity and reputation, these online hospitality communities help to alleviate the inherent risks of hospitality and ensure the smooth logistical and interpersonal operation of the hospitality exchanges. But the Internet is integral to these communities beyond logistics, surveillance or security.

In fact, these online/offline communities claim that using the Internet for hospitality in this way gets back to what the Internet was *meant* to be used for. These hospitality sites hark back to the early principles of non-commercial, grassroots, democratic peer-to-peer communication and community, thus fulfilling the original utopian promise of the Internet to unite strangers across geographical and cultural divides and to form a truly global community. Ramon explicitly denounces commercial uses of the Internet on his website, and Casey, the founder of Couchsurfing.com, was inspired to create his non-commercial site after becoming disillusioned by his lucrative career in software development during the dot-com boom. The not-for-profit status of the sites is inextricably tied into this formation of community, as the Hospitality Club website indicates:

The Hospitality Club is a non-commercial project. We founded it because we truly believe in the idea that bringing people together and fostering international friendships will increase intercultural understanding and strengthen peace. We do not want to make a profit with this site.

By rejecting profit models and commercial exchange, these websites reassert the "true" intentions of the Internet: to create a global village of strangers meeting strangers, sharing cultures and opening doors, hearts and minds. This utopian rhetoric can be found not only in the content posted by the website administrators, but also in posts by members, such as the following comment left on the Couchsurfing.com website:

This is not just good use of the Internet. This is not just good use of a couch. Essentially what we have here is humanity working at its finest. People helping people, with no strings attached. I've only hosted a handfull [sic] of times, but each time changed my life for the better. [...] Couch Surfing makes me belive [sic] that humans are essentially pure, good, and curious to know more about each other.

This comment, and others like it, reiterates some of the rhetoric surrounding the Internet and the virtual communities that were forming on bulletin boards and multi-user domains in the early 1990s, such as the Communi-Tree Group, analysed by Allucquère Rosanne Stone (1996), or The Well, an online community described in Howard Rheingold's book *The Virtual Community* (1994). Utopian thinkers at the time suggested that not only could virtual communities replace the sense of belonging that was missing in modern social life, but they could form better, more democratic and all-inclusive communities. In her analysis of online feminist communities, Irena Aristarkhova (1999, 2000) suggests that Internet communities were never going to fulfil their utopian promise of an all-inclusive global community, partly because community is by definition exclusive. She notes that:

> Historically, net communities have been based on protection and surveillance of their limits through the use of policing techniques that include censorship and exile of deviant users. [...] The net communities were not even in their heydays spaces for free access, play and negotiation. They were from the very beginning "governed" (another often-forgotten etymological meaning of the term "cyber" - *kubernare* as in "govern") spaces with clear notions of *propriety* (the "dos" and the "don'ts") and *property* (rightful ownership) (1999:17).

Aristarkhova argues that "closure is an essential and even constitutive gesture of net communities AND as such would always remain a stumbling block for those who conceive utopian visions of borderless and all-inclusive virtual communities" (ibid.:18, original emphasis). She identifies an algorithmic logic in which net communities are formed by cancelling out individual difference:

> In all gestures to unity (unify) there is implied a *principle of homogeneity*, whereby things are submitted to an equation that cancels out their individual differences so that a larger unity based on some chosen feature(s) of "sameness" could be *forged* (ibid.).

Aristarkhova goes on to explain that community based on consensus or unity only pays attention to difference in order to eliminate or assimilate it: "As such, the erection of a community is inherently allied to the construction of a defence mechanism which is vigilant to and exclusive of SOME other as foreigner and outsider" (1999:19, original emphasis). In response to such exclusion, Aristarkhova turns to Derrida's notion of hospitality to challenge the logics of fusion and solidarity within the formation of community. She explains that for Derrida, communities are essentially *inhospitable structures*. However, "lodging hospitality as a deconstructive *graft* within this structure of the community promises to keep it open to/for others. Hospitality allows communities 'to make their very limits their openings' and thus ensures that there is always a possibility of hosting the other" (ibid.). For Derrida, hospitality does not exclude difference, but rather "perpetually responds to the ethical demands of the heterogeneous, that is, of 'others'" (ibid.:1). In other words, Derrida's concept of hospitality intervenes exactly at the point where communities reject, eliminate or exclude difference by offering an alternative for thinking about openings precisely where communities would otherwise erect boundaries.

So where does such an intervention leave online communities dedicated precisely to the arrangement of hospitality? Do these online communities eliminate or assimilate difference, as in Aristarkhova's description of fused communities? Or do their ethos of hospitality and their appeal to ideals of global community allow them to remain open to difference in ways that other communities are unable to do? Derrida's formulation of absolute hospitality relies on an unconditional opening up to the unknown stranger. This unconditional hospitality is offered without knowing the stranger's name or identity, without expectations of repayment, and regardless of the risks the stranger might pose (see Derrida, 1999a, 2000). In fact, Derrida argues, hospitality offered to a known stranger or in the expectation of repayment is not hospitality. Derrida critiques conditional models of hospitality based on reciprocity, such as Kant's (1957 [1795]) notion of cosmopolitan hospitality. In reference to Kant, Derrida writes: "to be what it 'must' be, hospitality must not pay a debt, or be governed by a duty: it is gracious and 'must' not open itself to the guest [invited or visitor], either 'conforming to duty' or even, to use the Kantian distinction again, 'out of duty'" (Derrida, 2000:83). For Derrida, hospitality based on reciprocal exchange cannot be hospitality. Similarly, hospitality offered in the absence of risk can also not be hospitality. Derrida writes: "Pure, unconditional or infinite hospitality cannot and must not be anything else but an acceptance of risk. If I am sure that the newcomer that I welcome is perfectly harmless, innocent, that (s)he will be beneficial to me [...] it is not hospitality. When I open my door, I must be ready to take the greatest of risks" (cited in Rosello, 2001:11-12).

Contrary to these criteria, hospitality websites are instead based precisely on an economy of reciprocal exchange, both in the moment of the hospitality encounter and across the community as a whole. This reciprocity serves as a point of solidarity that bounds rather than opens up the community. Furthermore, reputation systems and systems of surveillance operate through the websites precisely to mitigate the risks posed by welcoming strangers into one's home. The hospitality on offer in these website communities is, if anything, conditional and contained. The reciprocity between hosts and guests in the moment of hospitality, and more generally within the community as hosts become guests become hosts, forges a global community in which members are open to each other, but enclosed within this economic chain of reciprocity and obligation. The reputation systems serve to further police the boundaries of this community, partly under the guise of ensuring the safety of members from each other by excluding or alienating "questionable" subjects, but also as a way of constructing bonds amongst kindred spirits; of creating an enclosed cosmopolitan community – paradoxically, a closed community of open-minded and like-minded people.

However, if these hospitality communities are not entirely open to difference, neither do they necessarily eliminate difference. The fundamental themes of the hospitality websites – world travel and hospitality – reflect a cosmopolitan desire for and openness to difference. In this sense, the communities do not reject difference, but rather "filter" it in order to allow the community to internalise the "right" kind of difference while excluding the "wrong" kind of difference.

The Paradox of Cosmopolitan Hospitality

Ramon's website and other hospitality exchange websites revolve around cosmopolitan fantasies of proximity to the other, global community and the "wealth of difference". Sentiments similar to the ones expressed by these couchsurfing members infuse all of the websites:

> Couchsurfing is another amazing thing that happen [sic] in my life. This makes me realize that people still believe into a unified world and that differences are our wealth and we are willing to learn from each other.
>
> It opens the door to unimagined adventures, and special bonds with people all over the world. Congratulations to the founds [sic] and all the people who contribute to the success of this global community.

How does someone become a member of this global community? What kinds of qualities or behaviours ensure that you will be welcomed into the community and get a "good reputation" once you are there? Despite claims that "everybody is welcome" (the Hospitality Club), it quickly becomes clear that this is not entirely the case. These websites implement several conditions of membership, a few of which I have already discussed, such as an ability to reciprocate both in the hospitality encounter and within the community at large, the sustainment of a verifiable identity and a "clean" profile, and/or prior inclusion in a face-to-face social network. Another important condition that members must meet, however, has more to do with one's attitude. For example, the SERVAS International website asks:

Are you:
Friendly?
Curious?
Open-minded?
Would you like to visit foreign countries and take part in everyday life?
Would you like people from other countries to join in your daily life for a short time?
Do you try to overcome your prejudices to communicate with others?
Do you believe that peace is possible if everyone truly wants it?
Then SERVAS is for you.

As this checklist suggests, these communities require their members to have a cosmopolitan disposition towards the world and, specifically, to difference. Members are expected to be curious and open-minded. They are expected not just to tolerate difference, but to celebrate it.

On some websites, this manifests as what Urry (1995) refers to as "aesthetic cosmopolitanism", a model that sees the cosmopolitan as a highly mobile, curious, open and reflexive subject who delights in and desires to consume difference. In other instances, this cosmopolitan sensibility takes on a broader political significance related to utopian ideals of global community and world peace, as we see in the quotes above and in the following statement on the Hospitality Club website:

The club is supported by volunteers who believe in one idea: by bringing travelers in touch with people in the place they visit, and by giving "locals" a chance to meet people from other cultures we can increase intercultural understanding and strengthen the peace on our planet.

Whether aesthetic or political, the cosmopolitanism described in these websites is fashioned through proximity to the Other. It is through encounters with the stranger that differences are produced, shared, consumed and, in the utopian ideal, transcended to forge a global community. But this proximity is risky. To be close to the stranger is to always be vulnerable to the stranger, and to the possibility that the stranger will be too different, or not different in the "right" way. And yet, being close to the stranger is necessary to define the community's identity: first as a community that has an exclusive and bounded space of membership and secondly as a global community – that is, a community whose identity is intimately bound up in fantasies of difference.

However, as Sara Ahmed reminds us: "While identity itself may operate through the designation of others as strangers, rendering strangers internal rather than external to identity, to conclude simply that we are all strangers to ourselves is to avoid dealing with the political processes whereby some others are designated as *stranger than other others*" (2000:6, original emphasis). On the websites, some strangers are internal to the community in the sense that they provide members with the wealth of diversity that makes unfamiliar encounters rewarding and defines the group's global and open identity. These strangers are seen as friends. A frequently quoted motto on the GlobalFreeloaders.com website is: "A stranger is just a friend you haven't met yet". The Hospitality Club refers to its database as a "World Wide Web of friendly people", and the Hospitality Exchange website similarly positions its community as a group of friends among whom

> common themes immediately jump out – love of traveling, of course, but also... our members' passion for food, conversation, music, outdoor activities of every kind, and sharing local attractions with other travellers. [...] Look at the sample listings to see the kind of kindred spirits you'll discover in the Hospitality Exchange community of travelers and friends.

Here, difference between people is managed through broader commonalities that unite the community in solidarity: "kindred spirits", like-minded people and an emphasis on common interests in travelling, learning about other cultures and eating foreign foods. Stranger-ness fulfils the community's need for differences that are consumable *and* communal.

The "favourable stranger", then, is merely a friend you haven't met yet. But what of the "hostile stranger"? How do "other others" contribute to the community's identity, precisely through their exclusion from it? Other strangers, whose difference threatens rather than serves the cosmopolitan fantasy, are invisibly present on these websites, often in the fine print. For example, near the bottom of its list of "Rules", the Hospitality Club includes the following items:

> Do not spam!
> Do not send messages to another member that are not related to the aim of the Hospitality Club. Those are especially but not exclusively requests for help finding work, apartments and visa invitations.

Clearly, people who do not already have the financial means to travel, a place to host other travellers or the political right to mobility are not welcome to participate in the club. This admonition hints subtly at the fact that asylum seekers in need of visas or strangers who intend to visit and *stay* (by getting jobs and apartments) are excluded from the kind of hospitality on offer here. Guests who might become parasites or enemies represent the "wrong" kind of difference; a difference that is not easily consumed over a glass of wine or a late-night conversation in someone's living room.

One of the most fundamental, and yet completely tacit, assumptions these websites make is that their members are already fully fledged global citizens whose middle-class status and "First World" passports ensure that nations will happily extend hospitality to them. It is upon this basis, then, that the participants can claim to be forging an open, global community, albeit one that is already closed before it even gets started.

Conclusion

I want to conclude with some comments about another cosmopolitan fantasy that circulates on these websites, the notion of "being at home in the world".

> The only requirement is that you open your heart and your home to hosting others, and the whole world becomes your extended home! What a way to promote

the values of world peace and cultural understanding, something that is needed now more than ever in the world we live in! (GlobalFreeloaders.com)
Bring the World home! (Couchsurfing.org)

Drawing on Dikeç's (2002) analysis of spaces of hospitality, and his references to Honig's (1999) arguments on hospitality and home, I want to ask whether the cosmopolitan fantasy of being at home in the world might be recuperated as an opening for hospitality exchange communities. To be sure, the rhetoric on the websites of bringing the world home and being at home in the world is underpinned by problematic associations of hospitality with rights of property and of "feeling at home" with a kind of white, wealthy, Western privilege that allows travellers to feel comfortable wherever they are. But what if being at home in the world were not about comfort, and not about rights of property; and what if we thought of the space of home not as static and secure, but rather as mobile and, as Dikeç argues, disturbed?

In his critique of discourses of national hospitality toward immigrants, Dikeç (2002:242) asks:

Isn't it timely to engage and challenge, as Honig suggests, 'the seduction of home', the seduction of the 'construction of "homes" as spaces of safety, spaces safe from the disturbance of the stranger'? Isn't it timely to consider the usurpation of speaking the language of hospitality in order to construct safe homes? Isn't it timely, in short, to reconsider the notion of hospitality, to reconsider what it means to be host and guest, to be disturbed, as Levinas once hinted at, by 'being at home with oneself'? What if being disturbed by 'being at home with oneself' turns into being disturbed by the stranger?

Dikeç advocates, instead, a notion of home as something already disturbed by the stranger. This calls for a radical rethinking that allows us to decouple home from stasis and mobility from disruption, and instead conceive of home as already mobile, already disturbed by strangers (see Ahmed, 2000; Fortier, 2003). As such, "being at home in the world" would refer to an openness that resists the urge for safety and comfort. It would embrace, instead, the risks as well as the positive possibilities inherent in Derrida's (2000) notion of absolute hospitality.

Perhaps another way of recuperating the cosmopolitan fantasy of being at home in the world is to rethink Kant's notion of cosmopolitan hospitality, in which hospitality is framed as the visitor's right and the host's obligation. For Kant, the laws of cosmopolitan hospitality assure the right of resort to the stranger; but what if the law of cosmopolitan hospitality assures, instead, the right to offer hospitality, in addition to the right to receive it? If we refigure "home" not in terms of conditions of property, ownership, safety or enclosure, but instead in terms of openness, mobility, strangeness and risk, then perhaps we can image a world in which *everyone* can feel at home and at home with themselves precisely by openly welcoming the Other.

Postscript

It has now been more than a decade since Ramon Stoppelenburg set out to travel the world, relying entirely on the kindness of the strangers he met through the Internet. At the time, Ramon's website was a unique and newsworthy project, Facebook and Twitter did not yet exist, and Couchsurfing.org was just one of a handful of hospitality exchange websites emerging online. Today, Couchsurfing boasts membership numbers in the millions, and is frequently cited in mainstream business discourse as one of the darlings of the new "sharing economy". As Couchsurfing.org has become a household name in many communities, the practices and meanings surrounding it seem to have settled into somewhat predictable narratives. However, recalling the days when websites like Couchsurfing.org or GlobalFreeloaders.com were just beginning to experiment with the networking power of the Internet reminds us of how undetermined and contingent these practices and meanings really are. Couchsurfing may be more mainstream now, but, as this book attests, it provokes ongoing debate. Perhaps this is because we see reflected within it a key question that shapes modern life: how do we live with difference in a networked society? Pursuing that question brings us back again and again to the slippery distinctions between hosts and guests, reciprocity and solidarity, inclusion and exclusion, cosmopolitanism and capitalism.

In this chapter, I have also noted that Couchsurfing.org and similar online hospitality exchange sites were made meaningful in light of a particular ethos attached to the Internet in particular, and to information and communication technologies more broadly. In many ways, these early sites were seen as emblematic of the pro-social and democratic potential of the

Internet, albeit in paradoxical ways. If anything, this debate has become even more contentious in the wake of recent developments in this sector. In 2011, Couchsurfing.org shifted from not-for-profit to "benefit" corporation status, and successful for-profit hospitality exchange sites like Airbnb have entered the marketplace. Indeed, the very idea that hospitality exchange constitutes a *marketplace* is notable, raising significant questions about the limits and possibilities of generosity, openness, reciprocity and cosmopolitanism in the contemporary era. Once again, Couchsurfing.org offers us an empirical lens through which to explore fundamental tensions that shape society today. Drawing on Bauman's (2003) critique of "liquid love", we might argue that Couchsurfing.org entails traces of both *communitas* – a kind of human solidarity that resists commodification – and the "dominant consumerist life mode" that treats human beings as objects of consumption. Here, again, Couchsurfing.org requires us to think carefully about the status of difference, otherness and strangers in this nexus of cosmopolitanism, capitalism and consumption. In this sense, it opens up yet another space for debate and discussion that takes us straight to the heart of modern sociality. As the chapters in this book suggest, Couchsurfing continues to prompt intellectual debate as we figure out what it means to be "together" with strangers in an increasingly mobile and mediated world.

References

Ahmed, S. (2000) *Strange encounters*. London: Routledge.

Aristarkhova, I. (1999) "Hosting the other: cyberfeminist strategies for net-communities". In C. Sollfrank and Y. Volkart (eds.) *Next cyberfeminist international reader*. Hamburg: Old Boys Network. http://www.obn.org/obn_pro/downloads/reader2.pdf (accessed 29 September 2012).

Aristarkhova, I. (2000) "Otherness in net-communities: practising difference in post-Soviet virtual context". Paper presented at Situating Technologies Symposium, De Balie, Amsterdam, 1 April 2000.

Bauman, Z. (2003) *Liquid love*. Cambridge: Polity.

Benveniste, E. (1973) *Indo-European language and society*. London: Faber & Faber.

Derrida, J. (1999a) *Adieu to Emanuel Levinas*. Translated by P.-A Brault and M. Naas. Stanford, CA: Stanford University Press.

Derrida, J. (1999b) "Dèbat: Une hospitalité sans condition". In M. Seffahi (ed.) *Manifeste pour l'hospitalitè, aux Minguettes: autour de Jacques Derrida*. Gringy: Paroles d'aube.

Derrida, J. (2000) *Of hospitality: Anne Dufourmantelle invites Jacques Derrida to respond*. Translated by R. Bowlby. Stanford, CA: Stanford University Press.

Dikeç, M. (2002) "Pera peras poros: longings for spaces of hospitality". *Theory, Culture & Society* 19(1-2):227-247.

Fortier, A.-M. (2003) "Making home: queer migrations and motions of attachment". In S. Ahmed, C. Castañeda, A.-M. Fortier and M. Sheller (eds.) *Uprootings/regroundings: questions of home and migration*. Oxford: Berg, pp.115-136.

Gibson, S. (2003) "Accommodating strangers: British hospitality and the asylum hotel debate". *Journal for Cultural Research* 7(4):367-386.

Honig, B. (1999) "Difference, dilemmas, and the politics of home". In S. Benhabib (ed.) *Democracy and difference: contesting the boundaries of the political*. Princeton, NJ: Princeton University Press, pp.257-277.

Kant, I. (1957 [1795]) *Perpetual peace*. Indianapolis, IN.: Bobbs-Merrill.

Resnick, P., Zeckhauser, R., Friedman, E. and Kuwabara, K. (2000) "Reputation systems". *Communications of the ACM* 43:45-48.

Rheingold, H. (1994) *The virtual community: finding connection in a computerized world*. London: Secker & Warburg Books.

Rosello, M. (2001) *Postcolonial hospitality*. Stanford, CA: Stanford University Press.

Stone, A.R. (1996) *The war of desire and technology at the close of the mechanical age*. Cambridge, MA: MIT Press.

Urry, J. (1995) *Consuming places*. London: Routledge.

3. Hosting Marco in Siberia: Couchsurfing Hospitality in an "Out of the Way" Place

Dennis Zuev

"REAL" ITALIAN PASTA[1]

Marco had one of those self-portrait photographs in his profile that are now easily taken by a digital camera – with an outstretched arm, in front of a natural landscape. I was not very impressed by his profile page (which only had one reference). In his couch request Marco explained that he could not find any place to stay in Krasnoyarsk, and therefore asked me to host him for three days. He suggested that he would cook what he referred to as "real" Italian pasta for dinner. Pasta is not my favourite food; in any case, I do sometimes cook it myself and it is widely available in Krasnoyarsk, where "pasta" restaurants had been present since 2006. But having "authentic" Italian food cooked by an Italian in my home – while not exactly being irresistibly seductive – was still a "nice thing" to do. I said yes and sent him my telephone number, but no directions. It was easier just to pick him up directly at the train station, as it would have been difficult for him to find our block of flats in the maze of the residential area.

Hence, my first couchsurfing guest in Krasnoyarsk was an Argentinian-Italian copywriter who resided in Barcelona. During the week of his stay I had planned to work from home. I had a deadline to hand in an article, and would not have a lot of time to spend with my guest. My initial motive

1 | The fieldwork for this study was conducted within the framework of the project "Conditions and Limitations of Lifestyle Plurality in Siberia" (2010-2012), funded by the Max Planck Institute for Social Anthropology, Halle, Germany. I am also very grateful to David Picard for his constructive comments in editing and preparing this chapter.

for hosting Marco, then, was not so much to generate a form of cultural exchange, but to help out this traveller whom I thought would arrive in a difficult location, far from his home. I believed that Russia and Siberia in particular were difficult places for foreign travellers to tackle without knowledge of the language or even a basic understanding of the complexities of everyday life. As a host, I intended to assist my guest with everyday things, including buying food and the tickets needed to get around the city.

The most successful couchsurfing hosts in Siberia usually have a good command of English and often other foreign languages. Many have significant travel experience, both within and outside Russia. Their conceptions of Siberia combine elements from their own travel experience with an often intimate knowledge of local realities, hospitality norms and ways to have fun. From this combination of personal travel experiences and the understanding of the social and cultural norms that regulate contact with foreigners in Siberia emerge specific forms of what I suggest calling context-specific "regimes of hospitality". Such regimes can be approached in terms of conventionalised rhythms of life, living-space arrangements and ways to engage with others. At the same time, such "hospitality regimes" imply a personalised way of treating the stranger-guest. For example, I personally consider my guests to be autonomous travellers who will go sightseeing in the city I live in without my intervention, on their own. However, the broader framework or "normative order" underlying my hospitality practice is similar to that performed by most other Siberians, in particular with regard to logistics. It is considered normal to meet guests at their point of arrival, transport them home and eventually take them to the station on the date of their departure. These three elements create a basic safety framework for receiving a guest in Siberia, but also in most other places. They constitute what could be called a general hospitality "interaction ritual chain" (Collins, 2004).

In this chapter I suggest using my own experiences as a couchsurfing host in Siberia – where I grew up and lived until 2009, when I turned 30 – as a departure point for my exploration of different regimes of hospitality that I observed among other couchsurfing hosts in several cities along the Trans-Siberian railway. The study includes a total of 35 hosts, observed through participant observation and interviews. Most of the Russian couchsurfing hosts interviewed as part of this study had themselves travelled abroad. Comparing their own experience in other countries or other regions of Russia, they usually knew about the hurdles that most foreigners arriving in Siberia were likely to face. This awareness often intensified their altruistic motives to help these foreigners and host them at their homes, treating them as people who had overcome great difficulties to access and visit them at "their" homes.

At the train station, the photo from Marco's couchsurfing profile helped me to find him. It had not been strictly necessary. He was the only non-local tourist standing at the platform; he was carrying a huge backpack with a bright steel cup dangling on the side. I thought that he really looked a bit alien. Until then, there had never been a lot of foreign travellers at the train station, and those who came usually stayed only for a few minutes – the time it took to change platform and move on eastwards (for whatever reason the preferred travel direction for most Westerners). We broke the ice by exchanging simple phrases of recognition. Marco? Yes. Dennis? Hi! We conversed in a mixture of Spanish and English. For many other couchsurfing hosts in Siberia, practicing foreign languages, and English in particular, is a main motive to participate in the couchsurfing community. Not so for me. I did not invite Marco to my home to practice my language skills. I had little interest in rediscovering my Spanish, and thought that Marco needed to practice his English. So we spoke in English.

The recent development of tourism in Siberia

In many public spheres in the Western world, Siberia conjures up many different but related images: of unsmiling people in ear-flapped hats rushing through forbidding temperatures from one snow-bound Gulag camp to another, warming up with the help of vodka, consumed abundantly in the company of reindeer herders amidst the tundra, with an occasional bear wandering by. It is usually represented as a frontier space, an edge of the world, obscure, bizarre, dangerous and generally inhospitable.

In fact, the inhospitability of Siberia's terrain and climate, and the historical legacy of being the land where people were *forced* to travel, gave rise to a unique hospitality culture. Very few people arrived in Siberia out of free will, with the principle motive to travel and visit the area's attractions. Hospitality therefore evolved within a pragmatics of facilitation and help offered to strangers. It was about offering shelter and security, and some food. While usually performed at individual and micro-local levels, the techniques, normative expectations and coping strategies inscribed in

"Siberian" hospitality have had a wider impact on the formation of Siberian society. The idea of mutual help has become one of the main ethical norms with regard to the accommodation of foreigners, hunters, fugitive convicts... and also tourists. The hunters and fishermen who roamed the taiga in search of game created a network of forest or winter shelters (called *zimov'yo*), which were used during the hunting season. This system still exists, and in some areas has been adopted by skiers, mountain climbers and other groups of tourists who venture into the wild. Often, the shelter is left unlocked, and one can enter and stay there overnight. The ruling principle (we call it the "the law of taiga") is to leave the place in the state in which it was found on arrival, and to leave surplus food for others.

Another social category of people who influenced Siberian hospitality culture are convicts. These were often treated well by peasants, without regards for their criminal past. One of the famous Russian exiled intellectuals, Nikolay Basargin, wrote, "Siberia embraced all without difference, as soon as a convict was inside its domain nobody asked why he was sentenced". Leaving food and clothes for fugitives, and even hiding them from the police, became a largely normalised practice in many Siberian villages.[2]

In Siberia and the far east of Russia, contact with other types of foreigners intensified during the 1990s. Following the political end of the Cold War, new opportunities arose for travel and border trade between Russia, China and Japan. The largest number of visitors on tourist visas were Chinese, mostly coming to do business, trade and work. The first Western "foreigners" after the fall of the Iron Curtain were Swedish, German and American Christian missionaries spreading the "word of God". They also went to Siberian schools and taught children English. In the 1990s, various foundations, such as Project Harmony and the Soros Foundation with the support of the US Department of State, organised school exchange programs and semester study programs targeting schoolchildren from Siberia and provincial European Russia. During the early 2000s, travel became an almost obligatory ritual for Siberian university students, and thousands of them spent their summer on Work and Travel programs in the US. For some places, like the cities of Vladivostok or Irkutsk, located close to the

2 | In the documentary *Kolyma, Istoriya Odnogo tresta* (dir. Miheev, 1991), one of the Gulag ex-prisoners emotionally narrates how people in Krasnoyarsk threw cigarettes and bread to the crowd of convicts marching along the street, despite the prohibitions of the military convoy.

borders, this opening up to new types of foreigners represented an opportunity to develop new commercial and economic activities. Other cities, like Krasnoyarsk, located far from these new travel and trade hubs, remained largely isolated in the middle of the Transsib, equidistant from Moscow and the Pacific. Chinese migrants arrived here much later than in Irkutsk or Vladivostok. Yet, despite the arrival of these new types of travellers, in absolute terms incoming tourism remained a largely marginal phenomenon limited to all-inclusive rail tours, the occasional backpacker, and fishing and hunting expeditions. Siberia remained in many ways an "out-of-the-way place", which in itself gave it a specific allure for many travellers, including most of the Western couchsurfers I hosted at my home.

To situate my personal experiences within a wider sociological scope of Siberian couchsurfing hosts, I have conducted fieldwork in three major Siberian cities: Krasnoyarsk, Irkutsk and Vladivostok. Krasnoyarsk, my home city, has one-million inhabitants, and was a major host to strategic defence industries. It has always had an image of a polluted industrial base, and was off-limits to foreigners until the *Perestroika* years. Krasnoyarsk has a well-defined and well-preserved historical city centre and – in my view – is a good place to visit. Yet, despite its unique geographic location on the banks of one of the world's longest rivers, the Yenisey, in the foothills of the Sayan Mountains, it has not so far developed into a tourist destination. During the 1990s and 2000s it was used mainly as a harbour for two of the most important package tourist routes, the Yenisey river-boat cruises and the *Sayan ring*. Despite its potential as a tourist base, its tourist infrastructures remained largely underdeveloped. The first budget hostel only opened in 2011. Many travellers may actually experience places like Krasnoyarsk as inhospitable because there are no standard hospitality institutions – not even an information point. Vladivostok offers a similarly gloomy outlook. A major military and commercial seaport, and the terminus of the Trans-Siberian railway, the city remained long closed to foreigners. Its tourist infrastructures are poorly developed. There is only one budget hostel, no information point, and few people on the streets who would be able to give directions in English.

The city of Irkutsk, located one-thousand kilometres east of Krasnoyarsk, represents a wholly different situation. The city has always been open to foreign visitors. Its veteran Intourist Hotel is still prominent, standing on the bank of the Angara River. Irkutsk is famous for its proximity to Lake Baykal, the largest and deepest freshwater lake in the world. Baykal-focused tourism is a major industry, with a multitude of firms offering adventure and expedition tours, often involving young foreign-language students as tourist guides. Irkutsk is also more foreign-tourist friendly. It has an information point, and maps of the city's attractions are available. With its numerous mid-range and low-budget hostels, usually located in former blocks of flats, Irkutsk also "beats" Krasnoyarsk and Vladivostok in terms of tourist accommodation infrastructures.

All three cities are located on the Trans-Siberian railway, which is in itself a major attraction for many tourists coming to Russia. Connecting Moscow with Vladivostok, and with a length of almost 10000km, the Trans-Siberian is the longest railway in the world. It has been popularised in the Western world through numerous travelogues[3] – the most recent ones being *In Siberia* by Colin Thubron (1999), *Ghost Train to the Eastern Star* by Paul Theroux (2008) and *On the Couch* by Fleur Britten (2009) – and films such as Brad Anderson's (2008) *Transsiberian*.[4] The railway journey has become a popular overland route for getting from Europe to China, and has turned into one of the main couchsurfing arteries in Siberia. The Trans-Siberian railway evokes a specific imaginary in Russia and also abroad, which is often related to the nature of contacts people establish during the journey. As Simonova (2007) writes, people traveling to Siberia by train try to learn more about the expectations and norms of their co-travellers in order to establish contact before the several days' journey begin. She also contends that travelling by train to Siberia is more personal and more contact-based than, for example, the trip from Moscow to St. Petersburg. The intimate contact between passengers in train compartments and the legendary story-telling of co-travellers have become a major signifier for the long-distance trip from Moscow to Siberia. Indeed, one can argue that the Trans-Siberian, which in itself becomes the first important contact zone for the couchsurfers coming to Siberia, is the first direct experience in and of Siberia, where social and ethnic differences blur (Stolberg, 2001).

For many Siberians, couchsurfing has become a new means to host foreign travellers coming by rail, and thus to create relations with the world outside. The Siberian hosts are typically middle-class locals with university diplomas, while the guests are usually middle- and upper-class white West-

3 | For a full list of travelogues, see *The Trans-Siberian Railway* anthology, edited by Deborah Manley (2009).

4 | In fact filmed in Lithuania.

erners from Europe, North America and Australia. Irkutsk, once the most popular couchsurfing city in the area, currently has 708 members, Krasnoyarsk 768 and Vladivostok 363.[5] The main constraint on couchsurfing practice in Russia in general is the limited travel-time allowance granted on Russian visas. Visitors usually cannot extend their stays beyond 30 days. Foreign couchsurfers and other tourists alike are therefore often forced to rush, and it is normal to receive guests who just stay overnight before making their connection to another train. Due to these time constraints, couchsurfers are often obliged to follow an "easy to do" spatial trajectory. Popular guidebooks like the *Lonely Planet* series often prescribe a largely standardised to-do list of attractions along this trajectory, which is to a large extent predetermined by the logistics of the Trans-Siberian railway. The relatively short tourist season is another constraint for tourists. The season for railway journeys is conditioned by the more favourable weather in late spring, summer and early autumn. Therefore, the peak of couchsurfing activity in most Siberian cities coincides with the main traffic of foreign travellers coming by railway. The fact that the period for potential contacts is relatively short may explain, at least to some extent, why the local couchsurfing communities feel less "tired" or "saturated" by contact with surfers. Also, the hosts' general awareness of the relatively poorly developed local tourist infrastructures makes surfing considerably easier. In locales that have had a longer exposure to tourist flows, and which have seen the development of a hospitality industry, the general attitude towards hosting strangers is noticeably different. In a place like Irkutsk, for instance, with a longstanding tourism industry activity, few couchsurfing members appear interested in actually hosting foreigners, and maintain their presence in the network mainly as a means to connect on a local level, and to participate in events.

The simple flat, built within a residential area of an industrial Siberian city, plus the residents of the block become the principle backdrop against which hospitality is performed. Despite the often exoticised expectations of their guests, the hosts usually candidly provide a non-folkloristic and non-conventional presentation of the locality, often promoting a cosmopolitan vision of Siberia stripped of its popularised, media-driven, and Lonely Planetised stereotypes. As Fleur Britten (2009:50) describes in her Siberia couchsurfing travelogue, "My point was that our memories

5 | According to Couchsurfing.org

wouldn't be of architecture and facts, but of personalities and homes. Couchsurfing gave a place the human touch...". She also observes that couchsurfing gave "soul" to unattractive towns. Thus, by becoming a guest in a private house it is possible to create an emotional attachment to the city – to see it not as an architectural or historical urban setting, but as a place where people live.

My home is your fortress: learning to be a host in Siberia

Marco was the first couchsurfing guest in my flat, and I had to notify my parents about his arrival. It was summertime, and in July few inhabitants of industrial cities like Krasnoyarsk actually stay in the city, especially when they have a *dacha*, a small summerhouse outside town. My parents were no exception, and were about to spent some days out of town. This meant that there was some privacy available for my guest in the living room, which is also used as my mother's bedroom. The day my parents were to come back was the last night of Marco's stay and, since my mother would be not be occupying the living-room, I suggested that Marco move into my room. I would sleep on the floor of the living-room instead. It is very rare in Siberian homes to find a dedicated guest-room. Most of the hosts that I interviewed were renting rooms themselves or lived with their parents. In one case, a host from Irkutsk mentioned that some of her guests were hosted at her grandmother's more spacious flat. Among the couchsurfing hosts I studied, I frequently observed the practice of entrusting guests to other hosts found either via the couchsurfing city-community group, or through personal contacts. In such cases, a host who for some reason could not host himself would try to find another person willing to do so, or invite other people in the community to meet other surfers in town, or otherwise spend time with them. Parents and other relatives in Siberia thus come to represent and perform hospitality as much as their (grand) children, who may be technologically more advanced, but who sometimes do not have flats of their own.

As for me, the curiosity of hosting a stranger at my parents' house was entwined with the wish to improve my "travel karma". I wanted to help another traveller, as I had often been helped myself during my travels around the world. And, since I was planning to go to Spain for a conference the following year, I thought that meeting someone from there would be a smart, practical move. I would already have a contact in that city, which would in turn possibly facilitate finding a host.

We had some food at home, and I made Turkish-style coffee. I normally don't drink coffee myself, but try to offer guests a choice between coffee and my preferred drink, tea. We discussed Marco's plans. He had no plans. Although not planning to be a guide, I suggested a list of things he could see in the city. I had a small stock of Russian-language city maps, and provided Marco with one, locating the house on the map. He had his *Lonely Planet* (Spanish version) with him, but it did not provide maps of the residential quarters, only of the city centre. It would have been difficult for him to find his way back to my flat without either knowledge of Russian or exceptional navigation skills. I did not want him to get lost in an English-language unfriendly (but otherwise safe) environment, and so I suggested that he send me an SMS on his way back. I took him to the bus stop, and Marco explored the city on his own. I worked until I received his SMS, several hours later. I boiled some ready-made meat dumplings (*pelmeny*) and made tea. I pointed out to Marco where he could buy food if he needed – downstairs in the supermarket. I expected him to contribute to the contents of the refrigerator. I later realised that Marco had no groundmat (*penka*), and intended to sleep on the wooden floor. Surprised by his lack of such an important piece of tourist equipment, I lent him my mat, which I usually carry with me while travelling in case I get stranded in the airport, on somebody's floor or in the open air.

The next day, Marco did not intend to do any further urban exploration because it was raining. We stayed in two separate rooms of the flat, meeting for the occasional tea-break. I started to feel sorry about what I considered to be my guest's "idling" his time in a place so full of interesting things to see, even in the rain. I tried to engage him in some sort of activity so he would not "waste" his time indoors. I had expected him to stay at the flat overnight, but not to stay indoors during the whole day. It was not that I wanted to get rid of him, but I felt that a traveller should be travelling and seeing things. I called a friend, asking if he wanted to take a "foreigner" on a tour – an Italian from Argentina. No, he said. Taking a foreigner on a tour no longer seemed to hold any attraction for my friends in Krasnoyarsk, many of whom then worked as interpreters or English teachers and dealt with foreigners on a daily basis. However, my friend eventually found another friend, a girl who seemed enthusiastic about meeting the

Italian young man and showing him around, despite the occasional shower of rain.

I didn't understand why Marco didn't want to go out, and was wondering if it really was because of the weather, or because he didn't know what to do, or just because he wanted to stay at home and look at photos in a book on the Trans-Siberian (which was in Russian). For me, and for other Siberian couchsurfing hosts I later interviewed, couchsurfing hospitality is perceived not only in terms of expectations of access to material resources, meeting a guest at the station or having dinner together. It is about mutual engagement and participation. Dinner and the organisation of visits are to some extent conventional means to establish such a mutual connection. Natalya, an experienced host, explained that the most important thing is to make guests feel positive and free, as if they were at home. She told me that she had had people staying with her who were not relaxed, and felt ill at ease. Even after she prepared dinner with a lot of "good" food, showed them around and told them many stories, they still did not feel good. She concluded that it is not the "big table" or abundance of "good food" that counts, but something between people that makes the contact between hosts and guests feel good. Darya, another host I interviewed, explained that,

> It all happens naturally with me. I do not know if there are any rules of hospitality or something. Perhaps I want my couchsurfers to feel comfortable, maybe not as at home, but more relaxed than in a hotel. And so that they would remember that they had a warm reception at my place.

In my interviews with other Siberian hosts, I tried to understand what hospitality meant for them and how they put it into practice. For many, it signified a type of performance that allowed them to personalise the contact with their guests and generate a specific form of memory among them. In this sense, hospitality works both on "templates" – like a visit to places guests could easily visit on their own – and on shared secrets – like secret places that have a personal meaning to the hosts. Because of the daily work routines of the hosts, they do not always have the opportunity to offer such shared secrets and personalised visits. In some cases, interaction is reduced to shared sociability: doing something together at home, like cooking or talking, watching a movie or having a party.

Fortunately for me, the tour the friend of my friend organised for Marco went well. Both of them apparently had fun, ate out in the city centre and visited some of the local attractions. Among other things, they had gone to the Regional History museum and to a panoramic spot near St. Paraskeva chapel. The latter is depicted on the Russian ten-ruble banknote, and many hosts use this banknote as a kind of visual narrative for this attraction.[6] I was happy that I had found a way to entertain my guest while still being able to finish my work. I realised the extent to which time and spatial freedom are important for both surfers and hosts, and how they mark different, often conflicting regimes of hospitality. In the case of incompatible time-space trajectories, hosts will hesitate to have guests even if they have a place available. Oksana, a couchsurfing host I interviewed, told me that she does not always accept all couch requests. For example, when having planned a trip out of town herself, or when she has business meetings planned, she will not have any surfers in her house. This is, she said, not because there is no space, but because she would not have time to properly receive the guest, to converse and do things together. She explained that,

> the sense is lost when the surfer just hangs around in my place and has a free bed. When I have plans for the day, for example when I need to get up early and the surfer has to leave the house with me, he will have to go somewhere, if he has no keys. Then you have to wait; that just adds trouble, especially when I need to do something fast.

When hosts are unable to dedicate time to their guests, couchsurfing does not seem to work as an altruistic provision of resources, but rather implies reciprocity and direct exchange. Unlike Oksana, I did not mind that I had little time to dedicate to Marco, especially because his request was above all about having a place to stay. Yet, once I had a stranger at home I felt that I was drawn into spending at least some time with him. As the language barrier made any deep-lying conversation difficult, the only meaningful thing to do was to hang out and do things together.

---

6 | The hydroelectric power station in Divnogorsk, Krasnoyarsk's satellite city, is depicted on one side, and the chapel of St. Paraskeva is shown on the other. These are two iconic attractions, which are also part of Krasnoyarsk newly-weds' one-day wedding tour.

Thwarted hospitality and how to overcome it

On the night before Marco's planned departure, I reminded him of his promise to cook "authentic" pasta. I made a joke about it, saying that I bought all the ingredients needed to make pasta and that if he needed something else, we could get it downstairs in the shop. Marco no longer seemed interested in cooking pasta. The fact that I had to remind him about his promise created some tension inside me. Maybe I should have just forgotten about it. But then I said to myself that as a guest he should remember what he had promised before coming into my home. The expectation that the guest will soon leave may make hosts more tolerant of minor inconsistencies or "broken promises". To some extent, the hospitality performed in the context of couchsurfing implies a temporary tolerance. The guest is expected to be a temporary visitor and not to stay for more than three nights, according to the Couchsurfing website. As a classic saying attributed to Benjamin Franklin puts it, guests – or here, couchsurfers – like fish, begin to smell after three days. Couchsurfing's ability to generate longer term forms of hospitality based on a more generic philosophy of open-mindedness seems rather limited. The choice of potential hosts will to some extent depend on what surfers expect that they will offer, including temporal availability. Since the time of hosting is usually short, guests are "forgiven" when they don't cook or wash the dishes. However, some hosts observe that they have to correct their guests, while trying not to offend them. Tatyana, a regular host, told me that she usually gets along with her guests, one reason for which is that they only stay for very short periods, and "you do not talk to a person for a long time". Were they to stay for a week, they would most likely bore her, she explained. In such cases she would wish they left sooner. She said that what annoys her is when her guests do not turn off the light and she has to turn it off after them.

To correct the "pasta incongruence", Marco and I went to the supermarket together. I bought more food and Marco bought a bottle of wine. My parents returned from the *dacha*, and the bottle of wine was shared among all. The cooking performance was simple and ignited conversations on a variety of things. We were in the kitchen, one of the main locations for Russian family socialising (Utehin, 2004), filled with activity and the smell of co-produced food. The way in which we together cut up vegetables and meat and transformed these ingredients into a palpable dish had something ceremonial about it. Our joint performance broke the ice (once again), and Marco and I talked about our leisure passions. We discovered that we both played percussion and, once the meal was finished, we improvised a jam session. Happy about the musical flows, which somehow created a connection between us, I made a copy of a tape with a recording of *darbuka* drum players from Turkey which Marco seemed to appreciate. In return, I learnt that making pasta is about more than just putting pasta in boiling water. Marco showed me how to use garlic for the preparation of tomato sauce. At that moment, I felt that my guest was "ready" for the next step in my personal hospitality "coda". I suggested that we go for a hike to my favourite hide-out, a place I deeply cherished, located on a trail inside the Stolby nature reserve that most locals would not know about. Marco accepted.

Giving access to secret places and dramatising one's guest's experiences

The next day we left early. I loathed the "conventional" access to the Stolby nature reserve, and chose instead what I considered my "golden route", more scenic and devoid of crowds. I like hiking through empty landscapes, and when I take guests with me, I do it both for my personal enjoyment of the hike and to show a personalised itinerary of my place. I keep some of the photos of this route on my couchsurfing profile, knowing that the vistas usually leave my guests deeply moved. In this sense, they also serve as a backstage presentation of my city. Marco was initially overwhelmed by the landscape, which was precisely what I had expected. He frequently sat down on the rocks to "take in" the views of the forested hills and river landscapes, as he later explained. Later on, we visited an abandoned youth summer-camp, which proved to be an exciting place for my guest (and me too). We both took pictures. The youth camp was a relic of the Soviet time, dilapidated, ruined and spooky. It seemed to correspond to the anti-tourist dreamscape researched by Marco and other Western travellers seeking "locked doors and demolished buildings", not visiting "places that are in any way desirable" (Kalder, 2006).

I had planned a full day's hike, and throughout the whole day I felt good about being a guide into what I considered the "heart" of Krasnoyarsk that few foreign tourists have seen. By showing Marco places no normal tourist would want to see, or even ever have in their guidebooks (like the abandoned youth summer-camp), I thought I managed to represent what I considered the "actual order of things" in Siberia, a balanced share of "anti-touristic" places as well as the more "boring" must-do attractions prescribed by *Lonely Planet*. Many hosts – including myself – believe that they can give access to a somehow more real, more complete Siberia than any guidebook. For instance, Anton, one of the veteran hosts in Krasnoyarsk, explained that, "when you get to somewhere, the tourist information or the map or something will not give you a full picture of what is happening in reality. [...] In most cases only the locals know about the stuff that is different from the usual tourist information". And even if you have some knowledge before you come to the place, it does not guarantee that you know the actual order of things there. According to Anton, a "full picture" can only be provided by a private host, whom he considers to be the ultimate conduit to accessing knowledge about the current state of affairs; a window on the "reality" of the place the couchsurfers are visiting. The academic literature on tourism and travel has convincingly deconstructed arguments such as those brought forward by Anton. While a powerful rhetoric of the local and its hidden, real "backstages" or essence does structure much tourist behaviour, it remains that: rhetoric (MacCannell, 1976; Picard, 2011). From a constructivist perspective, Siberia is first and foremost a narrative that allows people to identify, and identify with, a geographically and socially defined space. I as a host may have shown Marco places that he otherwise would not have seen, but I later came to realise that this did not make his experience "more authentic" or "more Siberian". What it did was personalise his experiences and subsequent memories of Siberia, no longer governed by a *Lonely Planet* guide, but by the interactions that I helped to shape. While I could not provide a "full picture", I provided what I considered to be a very alluring, though partial one.

Marco was neither well-equipped, nor in good physical condition for hiking. He bravely followed me until he thought it was time to go back home. He said that he "did not want to miss the train". I had carefully planned the trip, and knew that we still had plenty of time. Here was probably the strongest tension I had sensed during this first hosting experience. Did my guest not trust my timing skills? Did he not trust my local expertise? His anxiety left me perplexed. Marco eventually admitted that he was very tired, and asked if I was not. I was not. I had expected him to "enjoy nature" as locals like me would do, through strenuous hiking, solitary contemplation and little talking. My hiking pace and wish to show him as much as possible were perhaps out of sync with his desires. So, after a bit of scrambling up the rocks and reaching another scenic summit, we had a cup of tea, which I had brought in my thermos, and then started our return.

That day I felt almost like a hero – I had guided my guest on a secret mountain trail and shown him some hidden places of Krasnoyarsk. I felt transformed. Marco was a guest who had helped me to rediscover what I really liked about the place in which I lived, and I realised that I should not take this natural beauty and inspiring wilderness for granted. I had shown him my favourite part of Krasnoyarsk, what I then considered a secret "backstage". I felt that Marco saw Krasnoyarsk through my own eyes; although it was the natural spectacle that had amazed us, it was also I who had directed it, who had dramatised this spectacle, framing precisely the way in which he and I had experienced it. I felt like a producer who connected a majestic show of nature with an audience that had never experienced anything like it. Marco later changed his couchsurfing profile photo to the one I took of him during our hike, posing on a rocky outcrop near Stolby nature reserve.

Leaving Krasnoyarsk

To prepare for his one-day train journey to Beijing, Marco had to stock up on food supplies. I suggested that he go shopping before his departure and avoid buying "unsafe" food while on the road or railway. I took him to the station, as I felt that as a guest he should be safely delivered to the train, where my responsibility would then end. My father accompanied us. Actually, after my parents' return from the *dacha*, Marco had no longer been *my* guest, but *our* guest. My father had been asking him different questions with great enthusiasm while my mother was cooking dinner. After a short goodbye, we went home. Marco went eastwards towards China.

My first guest turned out to be little interested in my life or person. He also seemed not to have had any plan about what to see or do, except for staying in Krasnoyarsk for three days until his next train took him to Irkutsk, and then through Mongolia to Beijing. His trajectory followed that of most Western couchsurfers travelling along the Trans-Siberian during the peak season between May and August. Although we did not "click", I still liked his project of travelling through Siberia to discover places outside the chartered tourist maps, which I thought would help him and others to overcome some of the most resilient stereotypes of the country. I had wanted to show him Siberia not only as a cold, but as a cool place. I imagined that Marco was on a mission to fight against the stereotype of Siberia as a dangerous and inhospitable "nowhere". He was keeping a blog in Spanish, writing about his everyday life on the train from Moscow to Beijing. I thought that my mission was to help him in his mission – simply by hosting him at my home. Like many hosts in Siberian cities, I had wished to educate my incoming guest about local life by giving him access to my private family and friends. My hospitality and his journey through Siberia thus both seemed to follow a missionary logic.

While I did not really understand why Marco had spent so much time inside the house during the day, instead of exploring as much as he could, I still wrote him a positive reference (but not an "extremely" positive one, which I could have done). At that time, couchsurfing was, for me, essentially about the provision of shelter, safety and some food. I expected that visiting surfers would entertain themselves. Although I received many more surfers over the course of the following months and years, I frankly never had an "extremely positive" hosting experience. I progressively realised that this was neither due to language imperfections or the lack of common conversational topics, nor the lack of time, but to deceptive expectations that were part of my own regime of hospitality and related cultural differences. Similarly, Sergei, a popular host in Vladivostok, once explained to me that for him the cultural differences between hosts and guests were so deep that the short time of hosting allowed only very superficial communication. He told me that when he first tried to get into the community he thought that there would be a very profound level of communication. But in reality this did not occur, he said. In fact, most of the people who surfed his couch were primarily interested only in a crash-pad. Similarly, many guests who came to stay at my place did not manage to create any form of "emotional boost". They were always just "normal" couchsurfers; there was nothing outstanding about the way they saw the world or lived. I received my emotional nourishment from doing the things I always liked and seeing that the guest also enjoyed them – like walking through the Stolby nature reserve. I no longer expected deep conversation from one-night stayers with a language barrier, but instead became a believer in deep conviviality that was motion-based. We had to do things together to generate emotional flows.

Contrary to my somehow unsatisfying hosting experiences, being a guest at someone else's place was an absolutely different matter – even if my hosts only rarely had time to show me interesting places in their towns or cities. I tend to believe that being a guest is an emotionally more challenging experience than being a host. As a host, your guest is the main medium of learning, while as a guest you are surrounded by things to learn from: your host, his relatives, his rhythm of life, his flat, the city where he lives, the weather, the imagined "next stop". There is simply more emotion in motion than in being stationary. Perhaps the pleasure of having a guest derives from the power of imposing your own hospitality regime, your rhythm, your preferences and your residential setup, and through this imposition there is the pleasure of realising your "native" power – the power to tell stories, provide guidance and assess the time and difficulties in order to help the guest have a hassle-free journey.

After a while, I began to produce an increasingly standardised presentation of my place, anticipating the effects that certain sites would generate among my guests. Knowing the time constraints of some surfers, I even developed an itinerary to present the city in a single day, showing both the hidden, favourite places (which were no longer hidden but still beautiful) as well as the "ten-ruble banknote landmarks" suggested by tourist guide books. Receiving couchsurfers at home became a kind of break in the routine of everyday life and, for my father, an opportunity to practice his English.

References

Basargin, N. (1988) *Vospominaniya, rasskazy, statyi* ("Memoirs, short-stories, essays"). Irkutsk: Vostochno-Sibirskoye knizhnoye izdatelstvo.

Britten, F. (2009) *On the couch: tales of couchsurfing a continent.* London: Collins.

Collins, R. (2004) *Interaction ritual chains.* Princeton, NJ: Princeton University Press.

Kalder, D. (2006) *Lost cosmonaut: travels to the republics that tourism forgot.* London: Faber & Faber.

MacCannell, D. (1976) *The tourist: a new theory of the leisure class.* New York: Schocken Books.

Manley, D. (ed.) (2009) *The Trans-Siberian Railway: a traveller's anthology.* Oxford: Signal Books.

Picard, D. (2011) *Tourism, magic and modernity: cultivating the human garden.* Oxford: Berghahn.

Simonova, V. (2007) "Transsib: put v zhizni, zhizn v puti". ("Transsib: the way in life, life on the way"). *Sotsiologicheskiye Issledovaniya* 5:103-113.

Stolberg, E-M. (2001) Siberia – Russia's wild east. Some notes about frontierism, 1890-1915. http://zaimka.ru/to_sun/stolberg1.shtml (accessed 12 September 2012).

Theroux, P. (2008) Ghost train to the Eastern Star: on the tracks of the great railway bazaar. New York: Houghton Mifflin.

Thubron, C. (1999) In Siberia. London: Penguin Books.

Utehin, I. (2004) *Ocherky kommunalnogo byta.* ("Essays of communal everyday life"). Moscow: OGI.

4. Rooted Cosmopolitanisms, Deceived Kinship and Uneasy Hospitality among Couchsurfers in Tunisia

Sonja Buchberger

Introduction

This chapter explores how couchsurfing members in Tunisia interpret, adapt and reproduce notions of cosmopolitanism. Much of the theoretical literature on cosmopolitanism stresses a form of openness to self-transformation through the encounter with the Other (Beck, 2006; Nowicka and Rovisco, 2009, 2011; Werbner, 2008). This study demonstrates instead that contact with others – here manifested through initiating "cosmopolitan friendships" between Tunisian and mainly Western couchsurfers – on many occasions leads to social polarisation and eventually to the formation of a stronger "rooted" identification, in this case with a global Muslim modernity. In encounters with Western guests, the Tunisian members that took part in this study were initially seeking to be recognised as similar and close to their guests; in fact, as sharing a common European ancestry and global modern identity. This quest was in several cases denied by the Western surfers, who were often caught up in Orientalist stereotypes of the Maghreb and who reaffirmed the idea of a radical difference between Occident and Orient. This discrepancy led to feelings of exclusion among the Tunisian couchsurfers and, for some, a subsequent radicalisation of their positioning with regard to Western travellers.

My findings are based on an ethnographic fieldwork research in Tunis conducted from April to December 2009, during which time I worked with local members of the couchsurfing network. Although there were a small number of very active foreign hosts in Tunis, most of my key informants were Tunisian nationals of the urban middle- and upper-middle classes. Many were working as English and IT teachers in secondary schools, or as sales agents at various enterprises. My work focused on the most widespread type of encounter observed among couchsurfing members: the one between urban Tunisians and travellers from North America and Europe. The latter were typically university students or young professionals. What often caused underlying tensions during these encounters was the material enactment of inequality. The highly mobile visitors had the "right" passports and often tended not to be aware of the extent to which their travels were a privilege. This inequality between visiting and hosting couchsurfers created what I suggest calling "conflicts of reciprocity". These occurred even though the couchsurfing project actively echoes Immanuel Kant's (1903 [1795]) ethics of hospitality as a reciprocal exchange, based on the idea that the "whole community bears witness and benefits from non-monetary person-to-person hospitality" (O'Regan, 2009:185). Tunisian members – in particular those who face more difficulties obtaining international visas – experienced the hospitality provided within the context of couchsurfing as one-sided. Some even claimed "their" hospitality was "exploited" by guests who would probably not host them in return if they travelled to Europe one day (cf. Introduction to this volume). These scenarios, though hypothetical, point to the tensions that occur when couchsurfing takes place in an unequal, postcolonial context.

In this chapter I will explore the tension between the universalist claim of one particular understanding of cosmopolitanism and the processes of its local appropriations and transformations. It is this tension that leads to ambiguity when Tunisian members attempt to engage with a number of underlying ideals and voice a strong identification with place, on the one hand, and an insistence on the personal choice of identity on the other. Through intimate relationships, many of them strive to challenge "Islamophobia", and experience agency in the opportunity of immediate encounter and discussion. Observing the strong feelings of disquiet about and antipathies towards Arabs and Muslims held by Westerners, many Tunisian hosts seek to make a point about their identification as being related to their guests rather than being fundamentally different.

The term "couchsurfing spirit", locally also called *l'idée du couch*, provides here with space for strategic self-representation. Like floating signifiers, many Tunisian hosts relate to the relationship between Self and its position in the world. The "couchsurfing spirit" discourse confirms a notion of the self that users hold on to. It is considered as something you can have more or less of, and is closely linked with normative judgements. In both informal conversations and formal references on the website, a usual formulation for praising a former visitor is to say that he or she personifies "what couchsurfing is all about", or to call them "a real couchsurfer". Similarly, others can be criticised for not having enough "couchsurfing spirit". As I will discuss below, accusations of a lack of *l'idée du couch* are often interpreted as racism and "Islamophobia" when expressed by Westerners, and "Islamism" when made by Tunisians. But it is not just organisations like couchsurfing that engage in cosmopolitan discourses; there is a wider Tunisian self-understanding that it is an "open-minded" nation, too.

Imagined kinship and the politics of open-mindedness in Tunisia

The former Tunisian regime under Bourguiba, and later Ben Ali, consciously cultivated an ideology built upon the premise that the country was "open to the world". The ideology was part of a wider political endeavour attempting to attract future tourists and secure international investors. In radio speeches and national receptions, or in meetings with foreign politicians, both presidents promoted a pluralistic Tunisian identity. Unsurprisingly, this ideological endeavour impacted on national historiography, too. Hannibal, for instance, was interpreted as a "figure of world history" (Hazbun, 2007:27), representing universal values by building cultural bridges across the Mediterranean.

Linked to this historiography, there is a widespread narrative stressing that the country emerged from a "mixture" of cultures in the past. My couchsurfing friends usually proudly defend the idea that Tunisians are "not just Arabs", but the result of various ethnic and cultural influences, namely Andalusian refugees arriving in North Africa in the aftermath of the so-called "Reconquista" of Muslim Spain. "We have always welcomed everybody here. We did not only welcome Muslims fleeing from Andalusia, but also Jews", 33-year-old medical doctor Sabeur pointed out proudly.[1] This hints at another part in the puzzle of Tunisian identity: its Jewish

1 | All names have been changed for the sake of anonymity.

and Berber elements, which are often referred to when making claims to diversity. Whereas all but one of the Tunisian members I encountered were unfamiliar with any Berber vernacular, several members claimed to "be Berber". Djerbians in particular use *ᶜurbēn* (literally: "Arabs") as a pejorative designation of people from mainland Tunisia. According to this popular idea – that the Tunisian population is constituted of diverse ethnic influences – some members whom I observed in this study liked to explain different phenotypes that they associated with each of the nation's presumed foundational groups. Sabeur often directed my attention to the existence of "red-haired" inhabitants of cities like Binzerte, La Goulette or Nabeul, which are considered places of European immigration. Couchsurfing members rarely mentioned the background of Corsair activities and involuntary movements in this context.[2] What was stressed, instead, were things that supported their national imaginary of "open-mindedness" and "tolerance". At the core of their narratives was the long history of trade relations with Europe and (voluntary) migrations. In particular, Tunis was typically seen as a *ville ouverte* (open city) due to its longstanding history of attracting Maltese, southern Italian, Sicilian and French trading diasporas and Turkish civilians from the Ottoman heartland during the 18th and 19th centuries (Larguèche, 2001; Perkins, 2004). Thus, most members' imagined ancestry included European, mainly Southern European origins. The "West", therefore, is not only an "Other", but is constructed as a relative, a part of self. Linguistic borrowings, too, were brought forward to prove how illusionary this imagined divide between the north and the south of the Mediterranean really is. Sabeur, for instance, often pointed out Arabic loanwords in European languages to every single guest at great length, regardless of whether they seemed interested or not. One third of the vocabulary of contemporary French, he claimed, is of Arabic origin, which proves the long-standing processes of cultural borrowing. The idea of shared history and even shared kinship is a crucial point informing people's understanding of their hospitable encounters, which I will keep returning to throughout this chapter.

2 | Throughout the 17th and, to a lesser extent, 18th centuries the influx of people originating from the Northern coast of the Mediterranean was mainly a consequence of lively privateering activities. These Southern European Christians were sometimes bought free; sometimes they converted to Islam and stayed (Larguèche, 2001:119).

This pronounced claim to a collective, national "openness" (Arabic: *'infitāh*) goes so far that some of my friends stated that the literal meaning of the term Tunisia is "the friend" or "the open and welcoming one". According to this popular etymology, Arabic *tūnis* is seen to be derived from *tu'nis*, translated as "she treats you in a friendly way"; she is hospitable, welcoming, "open".[3]

For many Tunisians, notions of hospitality, friendship and open-mindedness are closely interlinked. Ahlem, a student of bio-chemistry in her early 20s, explained that Tunisia is more hospitable than other, more "conservative" Arab countries. She told me that the forms of hospitality practiced in Tunisia were not shaped by Islam, but that it was rather within the Tunisians' "nature" to be welcoming. Although there are several Koranic injunctions[4] about hospitality, Ahlem thought they did not play an important role today. Instead, open-mindedness is more of a national "habit" or inherent part of the Tunisian character, which includes the wish to "understand the other, even if the other is different", as she put it. Or, more accurately, she corrected herself, the people in La Marsa and some privileged neighbourhoods of Tunis are *ouverts* ("open"). In her reading of her differently classed national counterparts, less-educated people in "rural" areas are more *fermés* ("closed"). Her celebration of cultural hybridity and "open-mindedness" did not prevent her from expressing her alienation from underprivileged Tunisians, in this case. This also speaks to the frequent connection between cosmopolitan claims and the cultivation of upper-class status. Most local

---

3 | Here, many people assume that the Arabic radicals *'-n-s* form the root of the word, which links it semantically to terms like *'anīs* ("friend"), *'uns* ("friendship"), but also to *'insān* ("human"). In contrast to this popular etymology in contemporary Tunisia, it is widely held among scholars that Arab Tunis was the continuation of a more ancient Berber city, Tunes. Its adopted name is of Berber origin, with the radicals *t-n-s* being encountered in other toponyms of North Africa as well. They are said to signify "encampment", "halt" or "bivouac" in the Berber language (Mercier, 1924; Pellegrin, 1948; Sebag, 2012).

4 | Apart from the Koran, other Islamic sources like *hadīṯ* stress the importance of hospitality. *Hadīṯ* refers to accounts of what Prophet Mohammed said or did, or of "his tacit approval of something said or done in his presence" (Robson, 2012).

couchsurfers confirmed that being seen with Western guests or friends, for example, is often read as a marker of distinction among neighbours.[5]

In Tunisia, I found a remarkable curiosity about, and fascination with, relationships with "Westerners". It is this European element that people try to engage with and approach through their participation in couchsurfing, among other strategies. Through couchsurfing, day-to-day interactions with people from Western cultural backgrounds have become a reality. Most users now meet Westerners in person, after a long time of having only seen them on TV.[6] 22-year-old Adel, from a town close to Tunis, recounted his experience of moving to the capital for his studies at university. He told me how he was taken aback when he saw "blond people" for the first time, when he encountered "tourists" walking the streets, not knowing how or daring to talk to them. This preoccupation with Western physical looks points to the degree to which Tunisian subjects position themselves on the margins of the metropolitan world, locating the centre in the "West". This can have consequences for which kinds of people they would like to encounter through couchsurfing, and which kinds of guests would be less sought after or expected. Walid, from North Western Tunisia, explained this preference for Western guests in particular with these words: "If you brought an African girl home your parents would not see any reason for hosting her. It would just not make any sense. Why would you host an African girl?" This reveals the positioning of self at the margin of a centre (i.e. the West), but also the understanding that there are places even further out towards the margins, and an assumption that all tend to want to reach for the centre.

5 | This function of claims to cosmopolitanism as a marker of exclusion and assertion of superiority over commoners has been observed in various ethnographic settings (for Tonga see Besnier, 2004; for Australia see Hage, 1997; for shopping culture in early 20th-century London see Nava, 1996, 2002; Vertovec and Cohen, 2002; Calhoun, 2002).

6 | This frequent comparison of the looks of foreigners encountered face-to-face with actors/actresses on TV speaks to the debate about the potential of the mundane consumption of global media in people's living rooms to help people feel part of a wider global community and create a "cosmopolitan" disposition amongst viewers (Beck, 2006; Szerszynski and Urry, 2002, 2006; Urry, 2000; Schein, 1999).

What becomes obvious here is that societies differ in the extent to which they celebrate familiarity with certain cultures, while denigrating it in others. It goes without saying that this preoccupation with the West has all kinds of observable materialisations. People's consumption practices, their clothing, preferred music genres (e.g. House music, classic French singers like Jacques Brel, etc.) all attest to a strong influence from and aspiration towards this formerly colonial "centre". It also becomes clear when people talk about their "dreams" of living in Paris. For several Tunisian members from the upper-middle class, Paris is a place where they would move to – and some of my interlocutors had already moved to places like France, the United Kingdom, Germany or the United States only three years after having got to know them in Tunisia during my fieldwork.

But the more Europe is perceived as a place where you can spend a considerable part of your lifetime, the less it is considered "exciting" enough to make a good holiday destination. 30-year-old marketing sales agent Salman, for instance, explained to me in a café that he found Westerners "too close" to his own culture. He saw a more "exotic" Other in East Asians. Some other members shared his strong interest in Japan, which was manifested in various ways. People trained themselves in Aikido, attended Japanese language courses or even travelled to Japan whenever they felt "annoyed" or "humiliated" by the strict visa protocols for European countries. One member even went so far as to describe himself as "Buddhist". But during the course of my fieldwork there was not one single East Asian participant who came to Tunisia. Apparently, participation in couchsurfing did not offer the prospect of getting in touch with others and/or provide the chance of face-to-face encounters with these people as guests/tourists in Tunisia. Hence, only the most privileged could engage in direct encounters by travelling to Japan themselves. A third regional interest shared by the same group of members of the young urban elite concerned a number of countries like Turkey, Indonesia and Malaysia. Here, it was particularly the perceived commonalities and similarities with Tunisia, especially through their common "Islamic" character, which participants emphasised.[7] IT teacher Mohammed's travel accounts of heartfelt Indonesian hospitality,

7 | Turkey proved a popular destination for Tunisians, without any tourist visas required and reasonably priced flight tickets. South East Asia, in contrast, was visited by only two members, whose travels were closely followed and discussed in follow-up meetings, when photos were shown.

for instance, illustrated a tendency common among some to connect by belonging to a global Islamic *umma*. He shared the assumption with several other Tunisian surfers that there was a more immediate understanding, a greater feeling of closeness and familiarity when both hosts and guests were Muslims.

Is "Islamism" the opposite of "cosmopolitanism"?

After going through some world regions and "cultures" that Tunisian members are particularly intrigued by, and which become the focus of their attempts to "reach out" across national boundaries, I will now turn to the question of what people would consider the opposite of cosmopolitanism: the anti-cosmopolitan, the closed-minded or *fermé*. The majority of Tunisian participants would agree that "Islamism" is this opposite. An "open-minded" couchsurfing host, according to this view, lets (non-Muslim) foreigners drink alcohol and dress as they wish, without expressing any concern about having their parents see the person drinking. Several conversations and conflict situations observed during my fieldwork in Tunisia attest to strong criticism of local members who appeal to their guests to "adapt" their behaviour so as not to cause a stir or "offence" among family, neighbours or passers-by. An "open-minded" Tunisian couchsurfer, the argument goes, would respect the Western guests' "freedom" and not "spoil their holidays". Following this assumption, a "closed-minded" host cannot possibly be a "good" host, as they get into trouble as soon as the guest expresses the wish to drink alcohol. This becomes obvious in Salman's words: "What would he [a supposedly "closed-minded" Tunisian member] do when a couchsurfer [i.e. the guest] takes a bottle of whiskey out of his backpack? What would he do? He cannot host in couchsurfing. He is not a real couchsurfer". This speaks to the extent to which alcohol consumption has become a focal point of heated debates in the face of Islamic reform movements, and the wider antagonism between the left-leaning upper class and the majority of the population who came to vote for the Ennahda Party in the elections to the Constituent Assembly of October 2011.

This general understanding of an identification of open-mindedness or cosmopolitanism as the radical opposite of Islamic reformist aspirations is not only prominent among several Tunisian members; it also parallels readings among a number of scholars, not least those with a Middle

Eastern background. Sami Zubaida (2002:39), for example, writes: "Side by side with this cultural globalization [i.e. contemporary globalised consumption practices – note from the author], we have the most xenophobic and intolerant manifestations of narrow and religious revivals, of which political Islam is the most prominent in our region". Also, Kwame Anthony Appiah (2006), a prominent author influencing debates on cosmopolitanism, states that not all globally oriented groups are cosmopolitan; religiously exclusivist global movements that demonise those who do not espouse their singular truth are to be considered "counter-cosmopolitan", despite their transnational networks. Analysing forms of cosmopolitanism in various countries throughout the Middle East, Zubaida (2002) observes a certain nostalgia for the cosmopolitanism of previous decades, which he interprets as a reaction to Islamist resurgence and the "challenge of Islamic advocacy" (2002:40). As an example, he mentions the Tunisian film *Summer at La Goulette*, made in the 1990s. In this portrayal of life in a seaside suburb of Tunis in the early 1950s, during the time of the French protectorate, the audience watches a story of three families from various backgrounds: one Muslim, one Jewish and one Italian-Christian. The only villainous character is the rich and religious uncle of the Muslim family, which Zubaida interprets as an expression of the film's direction against the hypocritical Puritanism of nationalism and then Islamism, which put an end to this idealised cosmopolitanism of the colonial period. In a similar vein, the stress felt by some elite Tunisian members reveals this nostalgia for a long-lost, idealised cultural plurality in the country. Ibtisam, a 26-year-old woman from Tunis, for instance, told me of her parents' and grandparents' sadness when their European "friends" and neighbours had to leave at the time of political independence in 1956.[8]

In the last decades, a number of attacks on various institutions associated with "Westernised" consumption practices, such as a tourist infrastructure, have expressed the lively antagonism of "Islamist" groups against (former) regimes and their policies throughout North Africa. City-centre cafés, hotels and bars, all associated with alcohol consumption and the mingling of the sexes (with suspected sexual looseness) have been targeted (Zubaida, 2002:40). These tragic occurrences illustrate a fundamental disagreement about the presence of Western foreigners and "tourists" in the

8 | In that sense, the generation of users' parents already seem to assert cosmopolitan claims through their friendships.

region, about their perceived influence on "local culture" and about how welcome (or not) this particular kind of "guest" is. They are, in a sense, a very real, disquieting and violent reality in Maghrebi members' lives.[9]

Despite this frequent reading of Islamic reform aspirations as anti-cosmopolitan, studies like Stivens' (2008) work on Islamic women's movements in Malaysia highlight the ambiguity of several strands of global "Islamism" that can play a dissenting and critical role. The difficulties of drawing a neat boundary between open-mindedness and Islamism as an essential "anti-cosmopolitanism" in the region become most apparent when we look at key figures that are celebrated as early cosmopolitan intellectuals of the Middle East, but figures who those actors associated with politicised Islam also claim as ancestors of their reforms. Sami Zubaida (2002) explores this ambiguity surrounding Jamaleddin al-Afghani, a late-19th century figure, who was highly mobile, a polyglot, a member of a Freemason lodge in Cairo and an aficionado of cognac, but who is also considered to have been the principle founding father of the bipolar world view in which a Muslim-dominated *dār as-salām* ("house of peace") opposes a non-Muslim-dominated *dār al-h.arb* ("house of war", associated with "the West"), which is to be fought in times of Muslim strength. Although Tunisian members do not discuss such historical figures, it is noteworthy to what extent debates about "Islamism" as being the radical opposite of cosmopolitanism dominate discussions among both couchsurfing users and Middle Eastern scholars alike (Zubaida, 2002; Tazi, 2007). It is the complicated, messy personal trajectories of people like al-Afghani, but also those of several less "famous" individuals today – among them many couchsurfers – that raise pressing questions about what exactly our interlocutors mean by "cosmopolitanism" or its opposite. Phenomena of Islamic resurgence, pan-Islamism, increasingly mobile subjects and the online presence of Islamic websites and forums of diverse ideological backgrounds seem to challenge the theoretical position that there are enough similarities between diverse forms of "cosmopolitanism" to justify using the same term and analytical concept to explain this variety. While most Tunisian couchsurfers would actively use the term "cosmopolitan" to describe themselves, their friends and the couchsurfing project more generally, this issue becomes paramount in cases of particular narratives that do

9 | In 2011, one of the most active couchsurfing members in Tangiers lost his life in such an attack on a café, where he was sitting with his foreign guests.

not claim to stand in the tradition of what many regard as the "prototype" of cosmopolitanism: the Ancient Greek account by philosopher Diogenes of Sinope, declaring himself a "citizen of the world" ("cosmopolite").

Implementing Couchsurfing Philosophy among Postcolonial Subjects

As we have seen, there are uneasy negotiations about the meaning both of cosmopolitan and anti-cosmopolitan in the encounters between Western members and Tunisians, but very much among Tunisian members, too. It goes without saying that all parties involved share equality of perspective, with perceptions of the region being influenced by the long-standing vision of the "Orient" as a constructed, quintessential Other to Western modernity (Said, 1994 [1979]). In the aftermath of the events of 9/11, the frictions in Tunisian couchsurfing encounters took place in the context of increased global tensions and distrust of and resentments towards Muslims and Arabs. I have been in Tunisia off and on since the early 2000s, and have grown familiar with questions about the assumed hostility and rejection of Arab people by Westerners. Many of my encounters attest to the strong emotional tension this global configuration and dominance of Western narratives about the region causes in people (cf. Introduction to this volume).

The frictions occurring in the context of couchsurfing encounters in Tunisia thus speak to the ways in which some local surfers feel socially excluded in a wider sense from the dominant cosmopolitan narrative among Western members. As Pnina Werbner argues, cosmopolitan aspirations are threatened on two fronts: besides xenophobia, a rejection and fear of strangers, there is another potential danger, which lies in "hegemonic cultural universalisation which is homogenising and intolerant of difference" (Werbner, 2008:11). Both have considerable implications regarding cosmopolitanism by potentially leading to a defensive retreat into essentialised identities. This concern is crucial for a number of authors who reject the term cosmopolitanism in general, arguing that it means a distraction from power imbalances and is reminiscent of colonial claims to bring enlightenment to the "natives" (cf. Bhambra, 2011; Cheah, 2006; Hall, 2008; Kurasawa, 2011). These critics claim that the concept of cosmopolitanism, as it is often used in social sciences, is suspiciously close to modernisation theory, with its assumption of global convergence with an explicitly Western model. Therefore, following this argument, postcolonial scholarship, with its critique of Eurocentrism in particular, provides more adequate resources for making sense of our contemporary world (Bhambra, 2007). Working more empirically, Zubaida notes that the before-mentioned Middle Eastern cosmopolitan nostalgia for the colonial period tends to forget its imperial context, in which the "local" element was "inferiorized and despised" (2002:38) in the "false", hegemonic cosmopolitanism of colonial Alexandria. What role do these unequal power relations play in understandings of cosmopolitanism in the contemporary world? In a postcolonial context, which forms of cosmopolitan practice involving both Western and postcolonial subjects could not be construed as "Western hegemonic expansion in disguise" (Werbner, 2008:7)?

Relating to this homogenising universalism, it has been held that the tourism industry can pressurise host cultures to conform to (Western) tourist expectations (Robinson, 1999). This disputation can be observed in encounters and discussions on couchsurfing. Some conflicts occurring in encounters show that "failures" on the part of the "host culture" to live up to externally imposed expectations are negatively sanctioned. In several controversies on issues like over-charging tourists and gay tourists coming to Tunisia, foreign members frequently refer to the "couchsurfing guidelines" in order to marginalise argumentations by Tunisian members, claiming that they do not share, and have not properly understood, the "couchsurfing philosophy". Although the "couchsurfing guidelines" call for "respect and consideration" (Couchsurfing, 2012) when communicating with other members, many participants argue on the forum that this implies the "non-discrimination against gays". Several Tunisian users, however, openly express their resentment of and discomfort with (Western) gay tourists. Being thus accused of not living up to the "open-mindedness" of the travel community and the common values of its members, a number of Tunisians also attempt to use dominant discourses by referring to the "couchsurfing guidelines" in order to give their argumentations and justifications more weight. Framing the issue of homosexuality as one of "cross-cultural difference" between the West[10] and Islamic countries allows them to ac-

10 | As both the fascination about the encounters with Western couchsurfers and occasional preoccupations or concerns about "Westernisation" show, many Tunisian members take "the West" for granted. Yet, there are several who reject

cuse foreign members of exactly what foreign members criticise Tunisians for: closed-mindedness and lacking inter-cultural openness – a value at the centre of couchsurfing ideology. By advocating inter-cultural openness and learning processes, couchsurfing presupposes culture to be cultures (in the plural) that make people different from one another. Yet, it also emphasises the universality of hospitality and ethics – so it also reflects the view of culture as human culture, rooted in the Enlightenment conception of culture. It is exactly this tension regarding concepts of culture that takes shape in different ways in the encounter between couchsurfing members; it creates some leeway for Tunisian participants to challenge accusations of not conforming to (Western) backpackers' understandings of "open-mindedness".

What these conflicts reveal is the central role of the "couchsurfing guidelines" in policing a normative order governing specific cosmopolitan ideals. It becomes a powerful social tool to create conformity. As the ultimate challenge to test one's cosmopolite-ness, references to these "guidelines" in the context of heated debates between members from various backgrounds are the outcome of friction and unease between diverging cosmopolitan narratives evolving within what Appadurai (1990) defines as "ethnoscapes".

Extra-terrestrial Tunisians
Adopting a Rooted Perspective

It is not only the discussions on Couchsurfing.org that provide an insight into people's interests and the strategies of self-presentation they employ; user-generated individual profiles of Tunisian members offer this, too. Well before any offline encounter, the online profile page is the main means to initiate contact and let other couchsurfers get to know you. One of the set questions at the top of each profile page concerns "ethnicity". Answers are optional, not mandatory. Most Tunisians do not leave this field

an essentialised notion of it as a bounded entity. My friend Nadim works as an English teacher and is an active couchsurfer in Carthage, where he often shows foreigners around the excavations. He has frequently said: "I'm against this term, the West". But while deconstructing the category, he has also said he wanted to "lead a Western life with a Western wife". Clearly, the parallels with the confusion this issue causes among anthropologists are obvious.

unanswered, however, but use the question to convey some information or give an impression about themselves. About half of all Tunisian participants whom I got to know in some way or another use terms like "Arab" or "Berber"; several also write "Muslim" or "Mediterranean".[11] These are important nuances that illustrate the strategic mobilisation of ethnicity to create similarity (e.g. to members from other "Mediterranean" countries) or exclusivity. A considerable number, interestingly, use the question for self-descriptions like "CouchSurfian", "world saviour" or some other "fun" answer, like "extra-terrestrial".[12] Following a general postmodern pattern, the expressions used by this latter group of users emphasise individuality over nationality by making their country of origin seemingly invisible. But it is important to note that most of them simultaneously upload many photos of Tunisian land- and city-scapes. Popular images are landmarks in the capital, like the famous Bab el-Bhar at the main entry to the medina, or the panoramic view from one of the highest upscale hotels of the city. Other photos show Southern Tunisian oases with date palms, the desert or some white North Tunisian cliffs against the deep-blue Mediterranean. Some profiles contain extensive collections of photos of all kinds of "tourist attractions": landscapes like the desert or the beach and historic buildings and places. In presenting these types of visual images, a few of these profiles do not look much different from typical prospectuses for tourism promotion. The members themselves often pose next to historic sites, on top of mountains or hanging out with fellow couchsurfers in cafés. Many are committed to "show Tunisia to the world", as they say. As the omnipres-

11 | This emphasis on a Mediterranean identity, especially among well-situated Tunisians, was often touched upon in conversations with foreign guests. The similarities with Mediterranean cultures and the affinity to Greek or Italian cuisine was emphasised (e.g. olive oil or tomatoes), or members stated that "the whole culture [was] exactly the same". This imaginary does not only conform to the long-term identity policies of the former Tunisian regimes under Bourguiba and Ben Ali, but also seems similar to ideas circulating among Egyptian intellectuals and authors.

12 | Among Western members travelling to Tunisia, the most common reaction to the "ethnicity question" in the online profile is to simply leave out the answer or to go for comparable terms that suggest their non-identification with an "ethnicity", or their rejection of the concept as a whole. At the same time, they hint at feelings of belonging to a cosmopolitan, international network community.

ence of "local" images on the profiles prove, descriptions of one's ethnicity as "CouchSurfian" are ultimately not about removing any clues about one's feelings of belonging, but about asserting cosmopolitan openness and appurtenance to the same global network as others – despite one's "rootedness".

Something revealing about identification and the "rootedness" of Tunisian members was a month-long discussion about the role and function of "ambassadors" in the network. Participants debated the role of these nominated volunteers, whose task it was to organise activities for the local couchsurfing communities and attract new members. There had already been tensions about the issue for months when the conflict escalated in the Tunisia forum of the Couchsurfing website. The underlying question concerned who or what the country's ambassador was meant to represent. While he himself insisted that he represented the couchsurfing organisation *in* Tunisia, many, if not most, other Tunisian members considered him an ambassador *of* Tunisia within couchsurfing.[13] They said he should "give a good image" of the country and function as the "voice" of Tunisian members. A major issue he was asked to deal with was the non-availability of credit cards. As in many countries of the global South, credit cards for international payments are only available to a small, privileged group of Tunisians working for foreign companies in relatively senior positions. Yet, in order to become a "verified" member of the couchsurfing site, a couchsurfer needs to make a credit card payment which is then used to "prove" his or her identity. Non-access to credit cards makes it very difficult for Tunisian participants to access this privileged status as "verified" members. Some surfers were particularly concerned about the symbol of an open lock that appeared next to their profile picture for some years. Members who had taken the step of "verification" had a functioning, closed lock instead, making them appear more "trustworthy".

During the course of my fieldwork, I saw myself more and more confronted by an active antagonism between the couchsurfing ambassadors and several Tunisian participants. The increasing tensions caused some challenges for my continuing research, as the polemic led to the polarisa-

13 | This emphasis on country ambassadorship stands in contrast to Germann Molz's (2010) observation among her – mainly Western – research participants, who expressed a kind of "postnational individualism" by stressing that they were "ambassadors for themselves".

tion of members. A number of active surfers criticised the then city ambassador of Tunis for being of French nationality. He had come to Tunis for an internship and later decided to stay on for a couple of years. All ambassadors in Tunisia, the argument ran, should be Tunisian. In particular, French nationals, associated (or even assimilated?) with the former colonisers, should not be allowed to hold such a position. The conflict was, among other reasons, ultimately the cause for one ambassador to step down. It was clearly expected that Tunisian couchsurfing ambassadors could only be "locals", i.e. Tunisian nationals.

Various authors have brought up what can be read as both an organic link and commitment to place, while having cosmopolitan aspirations. Kwame Appiah (2006) has spoken of "cosmopolitan patriotism" to define this phenomenon. Mitchell Cohen coined the oxymoron "rooted cosmopolitanism", and called for an analysis of the way people belong to multiple circles of sentimental loyalty, having multiple "layers of identification" (Cohen, 1992). Working on the lived, every-day cultural "mixing" of steel workers in central India, Jonathan Parry (2008) argues that cosmopolitanism is not necessarily value-neutral in the sense of an ethics of accepting all cultures as equal in their difference. This proves relevant for Tunisia, too, where many users embrace different cultures and members from various countries and backgrounds, but who nevertheless retain a transnational yet rooted identity as Tunisians.

Besides a national identity, the "rooted" cosmopolitanism of some participants centred on feelings of belonging to Islam, which brings in another layer to Tunisian members' understanding of their specificity. One of these "transnational Muslims" was marketing sales agent Youssef, who constantly tried to earn some money in addition to his job to support his parents financially. "Before I invite a couchsurfer, I ask them by email to respect that this house is the home of a Muslim family", he told me over a cup of tea in his parents' garden in a suburb of Tunis. "If they don't agree not to bring any alcohol and dress appropriately, they are not welcome here". He went on to explain that he only invites non-Muslims after having "tested" them carefully to see if they would make suitable guests. While not many members went so far, more people shared Youssef's idea that their hospitality and "openness" were rooted in Islamic ideals. In support of their particular moral reasoning, they would often refer to Islamic texts. Several interlocutors, for instance, stated that they saw the diversity of "peoples" as inherently intended by Allah in the act of creation, and as connected to the mission to encounter and try to understand the Other. Many explained their motivation to connect with foreigners by referring to the Koran verse, "We have created you from male and female, and made you peoples and tribes, so that you may know one another".[14] This speaks to a form of "vernacular" cosmopolitanism which is neither particularly elitist nor Western: a form of longing to explore, and reach out to, the perceived ethnic, cultural and non-Muslim Other.

Personal exceptionalism and self-recognition

Regardless of their self-descriptions as "extra-terrestrial" on profiles, the overall majority of Tunisian participants emphasise a sense of belonging to Tunisia, while insisting on their individuality. English teacher and blues lover Latif was the only member who went so far as to assert an identity completely independent from being "Tunisian". In a conversation in a café in central Tunis, he told me: "I just happen to be from Tunisia in the same way as you just happen to be from Austria". By implying that there were no relevant categorisations of humans other than at the level of individuals, he mobilised a classical, cosmopolite rhetoric aiming to overcome categorisations in terms of nationality. What seemed crucial to Latif was that we only differed in our individual "characters", but that these differences had nothing to do with the "coincidence" of having been born in a particular country. All other participants had various ways to combine identification with Tunisia and assertions that this circumstance did not determine their entire being. Most did assert that there was some kind of private sphere of personal exceptionalism, as contrasted with the normative public sphere. This became obvious in conversations with foreign guests, when many Tunisian users attempted to establish themselves as "modern", "open-minded" subjects who were struggling within a "closed-minded", "traditional" environment. On several occasions, narratives about stubborn neighbours could serve this purpose, by members claiming they did not understand what couchsurfing was "all about" when they complained about the presence of unrelated women in the household of a Tunisian male couchsurfer.

---

14 | Qur'ān 49:13: *sūrat al-h.uğurāt: "ayyuhā n-nās inna h̲alaqnākum min d̲akarin wa-'unt̲ā wa-ğaᶜalnākum šuᶜūban wa-qabā'ila li-taᶜārafū.*

In one of his contributions to discussions on cosmopolitanism, Nigel Rapport (2007) explores this emphasis on the free choice of identity as a way in which cosmopolitan understandings can offer an escape from the situation. In his view, cosmopolitanism is something timeless that "humanises situationality", making it a lived condition. Regardless of how his approach, which presupposes a notion of a free, individualistic, autonomous self, can be challenged, Rapport's idea clearly resonates with many Tunisian members' understandings. Latif, for instance, insisted on his relationships with "cosmopolitan friends" as being a way to escape pressures in his surroundings. With foreign couchsurfers, he could talk about his doubts about Islam and his identification as atheist. Neither among his Tunisian friends nor with his family could he be "open" about these things. Nadim, another English teacher, also described how he felt better understood by people outside of his immediate environment over particular issues. His understandings of love and marriage correlated better with Western notions, he explained. Couchsurfing encounters and relationships offered them both the chance to live the "situationality" in their own way, gaining more options and leeway for personal choice.

There is also a tendency to assume that foreign couchsurfers, in their ambiguous role as "related strangers" who are close to, but outsiders from the concrete, contemporary Tunisian context, are more likely to understand certain aspects of their Tunisian hosts' lives and interests. This issue is worth relating to Hollan's (2008:482) work, who describes empathy as a process by which both sides can make of each other what they need at a particular point in time. In the case of Tunisian members, their relationships to foreign guests could become a means of "escape" – but not necessarily in the form of a post-national escape from a Tunisian identity. Rather than self-transformation, what many Tunisian members long for in their bonding with foreign couchsurfers is self-recognition and the fulfilment of their own sense of personhood. The expectation towards the outsider is to bring in this specific contribution in order to affirm and understand them. Literature on cosmopolitanism that has missed out on this subject would be hard to apply to make sense of the range of meanings Tunisians ascribe to "open-mindedness".

Given members' "rootedness" and the many Islamic references used when explaining their cosmopolitan aspirations, how can we explore the much-praised cross-cultural learning process that couchsurfing supposedly encourages? Western interview partners clearly had more consistency in giving a narrative account of "what they learnt" during their journeys and their couchsurfing encounters. The very idea that you can be transformed through such encounters is widespread, and feeds into the popular understanding of self-growth through travel. Being asked about this issue in an interview context did not require people to cogitate for long; rather, it triggered a verbal repetition of a narrative told to friends and family or written in a private journey diary or online travel blog.

Tunisian members, in contrast, tended to be surprised about the question and had to think a bit before answering. Some at first also misunderstood the question, "Do you think you learnt anything during your couchsurfing encounters?" and answered, tellingly, with what they thought their guests had learnt, or in what way their own personality and life had probably irritated what they held to be Western preconceptions. This has implications for the understanding of the conscious openness towards "transformation of the self" through the Other as the ideal cosmopolitan outlook. We need to refine this vision of cosmopolitanism when we deal with the desires and imaginations among Tunisian members, who most often would not share a conscious expectation of being changed through encounters. Their self-understanding is more about being "ambassadors", "teaching" others or rectifying their misconceptions by making them understand the closeness of Tunisians to Western culture – and ultimately their shared kinship. But where does that leave their cosmopolitan claims? While many anthropologists have described phenomena of creolisation and cultural borrowing, a few have argued that contact does not inevitably lead to these processes of hybridisation in Bhabha's (1994) sense (Ho, 2002; Pina-Cabral, 2002). There can be maintenance of difference over time. In a similar way, neither Tunisian nor Western couchsurfers prove to be quasi-automatically ever-more sophisticated, constantly developing intercultural "skills" as they socialise across social chasms that seemed unbridgeable before. There remain several touchy issues and situations that are likely to lead to conflict or misunderstandings, even after year-long active participation and constant contact with travellers.

Conclusion: Cosmopolitanism and Uneasy Kinship

If we attempt to draw a comparison with Ancient Greek cosmopolitanism as "world citizenship", one element that we find relatively little among Tunisian members is the call for democratisation of a new international order, or a call for global governance, in which all humans hold rights as "global citizens". The existence of (national) borders is not usually called into question. Many of my research participants did share these feelings of defiance against border regimes that they experienced as discriminatory and humiliating. However, most did not radically challenge an international organisation based on borders policed by individual countries. There were only very few persons who were committed to changing the current international political system. The real challenge to the transnational structure took (and takes) place on another level. It is in Tunisian members' conceptions and accounts of history that difference becomes displaced. Undermining the West-Arab distinction, they emphasise shared history and shared ancestry when they point to ethnic and cultural mixing.

The cosmopolitanisms developed by couchsurfers around the world are located in various ethnographic settings, with concrete practices (e.g. face-to-face encounters) and particular prior understandings. These local contexts impact on which notions of cultural alterity, cultural sameness and cosmopolitan openness can flourish or be discouraged. In Tunisia, the nature of cosmopolitan outlooks is highly contested, and the application of the term "cosmopolitan" differs between members. Some users' "rootedness" includes a strong identification with being Muslim, which is sometimes linked to the idea of using couchsurfing as a means to counter perceived misconceptions of Islam among Westerners. A few members, like Youssef, would even consider it a means to spread their faith and convince foreigners of the truth of Islam. Others, however, would see exactly these supporters of Islamic reform movements as anti-cosmopolitans. These inner-Tunisian tensions reflect the major ideological divide between the "secular" and pronouncedly Islamic parts of contemporary Tunisian society. What both sides tended to agree on, however, is a perception that the cosmopolitanism among some Western travellers can appear like a lifestyle, a "fashion" that people follow without any more genuine interest or "respect" for non-Europeans – which would include the recognition that Tunisians are not entirely different from them.

The frictions occurring in the field of couchsurfing encounters in Tunisia, whether they concern "gay" travellers, "respectful" styles of dress or attitudes to alcohol, thus speak to the ways in which some local surfers feel socially excluded from the dominant cosmopolitan narrative among Western members, as it is policed in forum discussions and in the "couchsurfing guidelines". The widespread accusation that they do not live up to Western-style cosmopolitan values reveals the exclusionary dynamics at play. It appears that it is these feelings of exclusion and of being "Othered" that subsequently lead to claims of shared ancestry and history as a form of alternative cosmopolitanism. Hosting foreign couchsurfers thus becomes an uneasy attempt to reach out to a part of self. The uncertainty that remains with regard to this ambiguous, imagined kinship is first and above all due to current distrust of and inequalities in encounters and Tunisia's marginal position in relation to Europe.

References

Appadurai, A. (1990) "Disjuncture and difference in the global cultural economy". *Theory, Culture & Society* 7(2-3):295-310.

Appiah, K.A. (2006) *Cosmopolitanism: ethics in a world of strangers.* New York: W.W. Norton & Co.

Beck, U. (2006) *The cosmopolitan vision.* Cambridge and Malden: Polity.

Besnier, N. (2004) "Consumption and cosmopolitanism: practicing modernity at the second-hand marketplace in Nuku'alofa, Tonga". *Anthropological Quarterly* 77(1):7-45.

Bhabha, H.K. (1994) *The location of culture.* London: Routledge.

Bhambra, G.K. (2011) "Cosmopolitanism and postcolonial critique". In M. Rowisko and M. Nowicka (eds.) *The Ashgate research companion to cosmopolitanism.* Farnham: Ashgate, pp.313-328.

Calhoun, C. (2002) "The class consciousness of frequent travellers: towards a critique of actually existing cosmopolitanism". In S. Vertovec and R. Cohen (eds.) *Conceiving cosmopolitanism: theory, context and practice.* Oxford: Oxford University Press, pp.86-109.

Cheah, P. (2006) "Cosmopolitanism". *Theory, Culture & Society* 23(2-3):486-496.

Cohen, M. (1992) "Rooted cosmopolitanism: thoughts on the left, nationalism, and multiculturalism". *Dissent* (Fall):478-483.

Couchsurfing (2012) *Community guidelines.* http://www.couchsurfing.org/guidelines.html (accessed 9 October 2012).

Germann Molz, J. (2010) "Tourism, global culture and transnational diplomacy". *World Politics Review.* http://www.worldpoliticsreview.com/

articles/7144/tourism-global-culture-and-transnational-diplomacy (accessed 4 March 2012).

Hage, G. (1997) "At home in the entrails of the West". In H. Grace et al. (eds.) *Home/world: space, community and marginality in Sydney's west.* Annandale: Pluto Press, pp.99-153.

Hall, S. (2008) "Cosmopolitanism, globalisation and diaspora, Stuart Hall in conversation with Pnina Werbner, March 2006". In P. Werbner (ed.) *Anthropology and the new cosmopolitanism: rooted, feminist and vernacular perspectives.* Oxford: Berg, pp.345-360.

Ho, E.S. (2002) "Before parochialization: diasporic Arabs cast in Creole waters". In H. de Jonge and N. Kaptein (eds.) *Transcending borders.* Leiden: KITLV Press.

Hollan, D. (2008) "Being there: on the imaginative aspects of understanding others and being understood". *Ethos* 36(4):475-489.

Huntington, S.P. (1996) *The clash of civilizations and the remaking of world order.* New York: Simon & Schuster.

Kant, I. (1903 [1795]) *Perpetual peace: a philosophical essay,* with a preface by R. Latta. Translated by C. Smith. London: Allen & Unwin.

Kurasawa, F. (2011) "Critical cosmopolitanism". In M. Rovisco and M. Nowicka (eds.) *The Ashgate research companion to cosmopolitanism.* Farnham: Ashgate, pp.279-293.

Larguèche, A. (2001) "The city and the sea: evolving forms of Mediterranean cosmopolitanism in Tunis, 1700-1881". *The Journal of North African Studies* 6(1):117-128.

Mercier, G. (1924) "La langue libyenne et la toponymie antique de l'Afrique du Nord". *Journal Asiatique* (Oct-Dec):298-299.

Nava, M. (1996) "Modernity's disavowal: women, the city and the department store". In M. Nava and A. O'Shea (eds.) *Modern times: reflections on a century of English modernity.* London: Routledge, pp.38-76.

Nava, M. (2002) "Cosmopolitan modernity: everyday imaginaries and the register of difference". *Theory, Culture & Society* 19(1-2):81-99.

Nowicka, M. and Rovisco, M. (eds.) (2009) *Cosmopolitanism in practice.* Burlington and Farnham: Ashgate.

Nowicka, M. and Rovisco, M. (eds.) (2011) *The Ashgate research companion to cosmopolitanism.* Farnham: Ashgate.

O'Regan, M. (2009) "New technologies of the self and social networking sites: hospitality exchange clubs and the changing nature of tourism and identity". In Y. Abbas and F. Dervin (eds.) *Digital technologies of the Self.* Newcastle upon Tyne: Cambridge Scholars Publishing, pp.171-198.

Pellegrin, A. (1948) *Essai sur les noms de lieux d'Algérie et de Tunisie.* Tunis: PUB.

Perkins, K.J. (2004) *A history of modern Tunisia.* Cambridge: Cambridge University Press.

Pina-Cabral, J. de (2002) *Between China and Europe: person, culture and emotion in Macao.* New York: Continuum.

Rapport, N. (2007) "An outline for cosmopolitan study: reclaiming the human through introspection". *Current Anthropology* 48(2):257-283.

Robinson, M. (1999) "Cultural conflicts in tourism: inevitability and inequality". In P. Boniface and M. Robinson (eds.) *Tourism and cultural conflicts.* Wallingford: CABI, pp.1-32.

Robson, J. (2012) "H.adīth". In P. Bearman et al. (eds.) *Encyclopaedia of Islam.* Second Edition. Brill Online. http://www.brillonline.nl.ezproxy.soas.ac.uk/subscriber/uid=1415/entry?entry=islam_COM-0248 (accessed 29 March 2012).

Said, E.W. (1994 [1979]) *Orientalism.* Reprinted with a new afterword. Harmondsworth: Penguin.

Schein, L. (1999) "Of cargo and satellites: imagined cosmopolitanism". *Postcolonial Studies: Culture, Politics, Economy* 2(3):345-375.

Sebag, P. (2012) "Tūnis". In P. Bearman et al. (eds.) *Encyclopaedia of Islam.* Second Edition. Brill Online. http://www.brillonline.nl/subscriber/entry?entry=islam_SIM-7630 (accessed 13 February 2012).

Stivens, M. (2008) "Gender, rights and cosmopolitanisms". In P. Werbner (ed.) *Anthropology and the new cosmopolitanism: rooted, feminist and vernacular perspectives.* New York: Berg, pp.87-110.

Szerszynski, B. and Urry, J. (2002) "Cultures of cosmopolitanism". *The Sociological Review* 50(4):461-481.

Szerszynski, B. and Urry, J. (2006) "Visuality, mobility and the cosmopolitan: inhabiting the world from afar". *The British Journal of Sociology* 57(1):113-131.

Tazi, N. (2007) "Is it possible to be both a cosmopolitan and a Muslim?" In S. Ossman (ed.) *Places we share: migration, subjectivity, and global mobility.* Lanham: Lexington Books, pp.17-26.

Urry, J. (2000) "The global media and cosmopolitanism". Paper at the Transnational America Conference, Bavarian American Academy, Munich. http://www.lancs.ac.uk/fass/sociology/papers/urry-global-media.pdf (accessed 4 March 2012).

Vertovec, S. and Cohen, R. (2002) "Introduction: conceiving cosmopolitanism". In S. Vertovec and R. Cohen (eds.) *Conceiving cosmopolitanism: theory, context and practice.* Oxford: Oxford University Press, pp.1-22.

Werbner, P. (ed.) (2008) *Anthropology and the New Cosmopolitanism: rooted, feminist and vernacular perspectives.* ASA Monographs. New York: Berg.

Werbner, P. (2008) "Introduction: towards a New Cosmopolitan Anthropology". In P. Werbner (ed.) *Anthropology and the new cosmopolitanism: rooted, feminist and vernacular perspectives.* ASA Monographs. New York: Berg, pp.1-29.

Zubaida, S. (2002) "Middle Eastern experiences of cosmopolitanism". In S. Vertovec and R. Cohen (eds.) *Conceiving cosmopolitanism: theory, context, and practice.* Oxford: Oxford University Press, pp.32-41.

5. Learning to Perform the Exotic: Cosmopolitan Imagination, Participation and Self-Transformation among Taiwanese Couchsurfers

De-Jung Chen

INTRODUCTION[1]

The complexification of transnational connections and interactions that mark the global age has come to challenge the dominant narratives of national sovereignty and geographical boundaries that define individual belonging (Hannerz, 1990). In this context, people have come to realise that they do not live and act solely in the self-enclosed spaces of national states and their respective national societies (Beck, 2000; Dower, 2008; Nowicka and Rovisco, 2009). One response to the weakening of nationalist metanarratives has been a renewed interest in the concept of cosmopolitanism. However, it has been observed that this concept reflects above all a "Western" perspective upon the world (Beck, 2004, 2006, 2011). While cosmopolitan discourse tends to encompass the world, it does not automatically represent the world and how it is being viewed by all people that inhabit it. Some authors suggest that cosmopolitanism promotes a specific aesthetic

1 | This study is part of my PhD project „Mobilities in a Cosmopolitan World - CouchSurfing Experiences in the Netherlands and Taiwan", which is supported by Prof. Robert Kloosterman and Amsterdam Institute for Social Science Research (AISSR). Besides Prof. Kloosterman, I want to thank Dr. Pieter Terhorst, Professor Geselinde Kuipers and Dr. Jennie Germann Molz for their useful and critical suggestions for this study, and also thank Dr. David Picard for editing and improving this chapter.

stance involving an intellectual taste for different and diverse cultural experiences at individual level (Roudometof, 2005; Werbner, 2008; Regev, 2007). In this sense it has become a "good" produced and exchanged in modern consumer society, where the act of consuming "other" cultures transforms modern consumers into "everyday cosmopolitans" (Beck, 2006; Haldrup and Larsen, 2010). Where commercial exchanges and acquisitions become easily accessible means to participate in the realms of global society, buying into the signs and ambiences of the cosmopolitan aesthetic can be seen as acts of individual consumption. In this sense, consumption becomes a cosmopolitan practice par excellence.

In this chapter I will explore how Taiwanese couchsurfers, by hosting, travelling and meeting up with foreigners, imagine, learn and adapt the concept of cosmopolitanism, and by these means undergo a process of self-transformation. My research is developed along with a series of questions: how do Taiwanese couchsurfers interact with people from other countries and with other cultures? Through which means, forms and narratives do they perform "their" identity? What do they learn from cross-cultural interactions enabled through couchsurfing? To respond to these questions, I have carried out a series of 21 interviews with Taiwanese couchsurfers, whom I met via the couchsurfing website. Eight were males and 13 females, and their age ranged between 21 and 60. Furthermore, I organised a group workshop with 18 couchsurfers from Taiwan to discuss their couchsurfing experiences. A key question I suggested for debate was what makes a "good" host or guest in couchsurfing. Based on these interviews, and the discussions that took place during the workshop, I will first explore the general attitudes among the samples with regard to "other cultures". The interviews and workshops will also serve to facilitate a study of how these couchsurfers experienced their interactions with couchsurfers from other countries, and provide an investigation of forms of self-transformation observed among the sample. Self-transformation is defined here as a learning process of acquiring and personalising a cosmopolitan ability and identity.

Couchsurfing cosmopolitanism as selectively open-minded

Most of the Taiwanese couchsurfers that took part in this study considered couchsurfing above all in terms of the cosmopolitan atmosphere it creates, and the open-minded attitude it propagates among its members. Rose, for instance, a 24-year-old female Taiwanese couchsurfer, said she believed that couchsurfing attracts people who are open-minded and easy-going, and who love different cultures. She explained that, "if you are a conservative person, you will never participate in this project; because the members are all strangers. Normally couchsurfers love travel and adventure in different countries. And most of them are also easy-going".

Rose's discourse reflects a wider commonly held view among most Taiwanese couchsurfers that the community is above all about being "open-minded", about having an open attitude toward new things, strangers and different cultures. While couchsurfing encourages cross-cultural interactions and understanding among members, it also helps to attract people who share the same values and characteristics to participate in this project. As Germann Molz (2007:66) argues, a cosmopolitan disposition of openness to difference actually serves to delimit a bounded community of "like-minded" but diverse individuals. Yet, not all couchsurfers "feel" like-minded; for many, becoming like-minded is a learning process. Hua, for example, a 21-year-old female surfer, explained that she was surprised by the forms of "easy" interactions among total strangers she experienced during her first couchsurfing experience in Europe:

> I observed their (my host's and another couchsurfer's) interaction; it seemed that they had known each other for a long time, but that day was exactly the first time they met. It was marvellous... They were really easy-going. One of them cooked a new French dish; then he announced on the couchsurfing website that he'd invite other couchsurfers, and some couchsurfers just came. But they never knew each other or even met each other before! It's easy for them to invite strangers to have dinner at home. They are very open-minded and willing to make friends. I think if we [i.e. Taiwanese] were them, we would feel uneasy about inviting strangers home, and would not know how to behave.

Here, and in various other parts of our interview, Hua consistently discussed her observations through an "us-them" dichotomy. Couchsurfing, she appeared to imagine, has its own culture and atmosphere which is shared by similar types of people and communities. Hua didn't seem to think that she and other Taiwanese were part of this community, even though she had been an active couchsurfing member for several years. Despite feeling this "culture gap" between herself and most of the couchsurfing community, Hua still expressed her willingness to participate in the practice. She explained that, in order to be part of "them", she tried to behave "not so Taiwanese" – for example, she didn't speak or behave as politely as she did in Taiwan. When interacting with foreigners, she switched to another mode of communication:

> I get along with friends in Taiwan in a certain mode, and I switch to another one when I travel abroad and meet new [couchsurfing] friends... I change my attitude and behaviour unconsciously at that moment, but I know that I feel like [I want] to be part of them immediately. I don't want to behave very politely or punctiliously like a typical Taiwanese when I interact with foreign couchsurfers. Because I feel that we Taiwanese or Chinese are too courteous for foreigners; for example, we always say sorry or prepare gifts for others. They think we are strange.

The "self-transformation" among Taiwanese couchsurfers does not only describe a process of acquiring a cosmopolitan attitude towards strangers (Nowicka and Rovisco, 2009), but also a process of self-reflection about one's own culture (Kennedy, 2009) – seen through a stranger's eyes. Hua realised that the courteous attitudes and behaviours that Taiwanese find normal to govern their interactions often appear strange to foreign couchsurfers. In her encounters, she started to switch to another more direct and "open" mode, which she considers "less Taiwanese". By that means, by learning and adopting a cosmopolitan attitude, she progressively transformed into what she considers a cosmopolite. She partly and situationally became part of "them".

Becoming conscious about the socially constructed nature of nation-based culture leads not only to a process of self-reflection, but also to the realisation that the concept of national culture is embedded in powerful narratives and stereotypes that surface in the social field of couchsurfing practice. Ru, a 26-year-old female surfer, explained how she was subjected to such stereotypes when surfing in Europe:

> I stayed with a Belgian host. [...] Because I don't want to be considered as a free-loader or lazy guest, I always said I was willing to help to do the dishes or something else. Also, I respected her as the host, so I always asked her when I needed to do something in her house or borrow her stuff. I tried to be as courteous as possible. However, my host told me directly, "You make me uncomfortable". Even though she said I was the first Asian she had hosted. But she may have had some travel experiences that made her feel that, "it seems you Asian are used to wear

masks; you are apparently happy and smiling all the time. But why? You don't have to behave like that". I guess her prejudice about Asians made her uncomfortable with my behaviour.

Ru directly confronted the widely held Western stereotype about Asians as overly polite people who hide their presumably "real" tastes and intentions behind masks when not conforming to an ideal of personal openness and transparency. While the use of stereotypes is observed in most social interactions, especially where these involve contact between strangers, at the same time such stereotypes often create prejudice and lead to the sidelining and exclusion of people associated with certain cultures. This presence of stereotypes in actual couchsurfing practice constitutes an inherent contradiction with regard to the cosmopolitan discourse – which instead claims to embody equality and respect. Hence, while most Taiwanese couchsurfers define cosmopolitanism in terms of an open-minded attitude to difference, they also recognise the limits of this philosophy to generate open-mindedness in practice. Often, cosmopolitanism is instead considered as a selective attribute of a community open to people with certain characteristics and closed to others. In order to be part of this community, many non-Western couchsurfers, including the Taiwanese who took part in this study, explained that they have to sense which cultural characteristics are accepted and which aren't by the Western majority, from whose perspective Taiwanese couchsurfers experience the interwoven process of self-reflection in nation-based culture and self-transformation from being local to cosmopolitan.

The cosmopolitan taste for the "authentic"

The couchsurfing website propagates cosmopolitan imaginations for both hosts and surfers. To the hosts, couchsurfing promises a cosmopolitan life based upon diverse cultural experiences at home; to the surfers, couchsurfing offers authentic local experiences of the places they visit (Chen, 2012). The cosmopolitan imagination of living/travelling with international friends around the world is accepted and expected by most Taiwanese hosts and surfers. They are primary motivations to participate in the couchsurfing community. Starkid, a 30-year-old male surfer, was one of them. He participated because, so he explained, he was eager to make new friends from around the world:

> The essence of couchsurfing is not searching for free accommodation, but knowing different cultures and making friends. I love to make friends from different countries and with different cultural backgrounds. [...] When we start to work, in our daily life we only interact with our colleagues or with friends from past schools sometimes. Couchsurfing gives me the chance to know new friends from different countries. I really like these new friends in my life.

For Starkid, couchsurfing allowed him to fulfil a dream of a cosmopolitan life. He took the photo of every surfer who stayed at his place, and displayed all of these photos on the wall of his room. Via this wall of photos, he created a display of his cosmopolitan life as well as his strong identity of being part of the couchsurfing community. These cosmopolitan imaginations seem more connected to an individualised identity, in a way disconnected from any claims to global citizenship as a person who enjoys a life in contact with different cultures and people. Similarly, Moon, a 25-year-old male writer of film scripts, participated in couchsurfing in order to meet people with different cultural backgrounds and stories. He considered mobility from the perspective of his immobility, where movement and travel imaginations were created through the hosting of guests at his home. For him, hosting surfers and talking to them was a source of inspiration. It allowed him to come up with new plots and storylines all the time:

> So, I participate in other people's trips in my city. [...] This is a relative concept. For example, when a car is passing by a tree, the car is moving and the tree is standing still. Yet, from the perspective of the car it is the tree that is moving. If I imagine that I am the tree, I can stay in my place and travel by hosting couchsurfers. Stories, people and travel experience would come straight to my door. All I have to do is wait for them at my place.

Many Taiwanese surfers embrace different forms of cosmopolitan imagination during their trips, for instance by searching for "authentic local cultures" in different places. In line with a frequently made claim by the couchsurfing community, this quest for the "cultural real" becomes part of a wider cosmopolitan attitude, often constructed in opposition to the presumably idiosyncratic nature of mass-tourism experience. The dualism in Western tourism discourse between travellers and tourists has been discussed for decades in tourism studies. Boorstin was the first scholar to criticise tourists, who, he claimed, cannot experience reality directly but thrive on "pseudo events" arranged by the tourist industry. Following Boorstin, other scholars, such as Turner and Ash, argue that the tourism industry oversimplifies local culture or indigenous art into tourist kitsch in order to respond to the taste of mass-tourists (Urry, 2002). Most Taiwanese couchsurfers realise the stigma the couchsurfing community associates with being a "tourist". 24-year-old female surfer Jasmine explained that before knowing couchsurfing, she didn't know how to travel and was "just a stupid tourist". Another interviewee, 24-year-old Rose, emphasised the idea that staying with local people allowed her to experience "real local life". She said that she didn't want to be a tourist, so she usually followed the habits of local people, for example to the restaurants where they usually eat. "It's funny", she explained, "don't you feel that visiting a city should be like this? Experience the real local life! Moreover, I stay in different hosts' places, which means I would experience different people's life in the same city and see the different aspects of this city".

For most Taiwanese surfers, the practice of copying locals or staying at the places where local people stay seemed a means to access the presumed "authenticity" of local life. It constituted a key motivation to participate in couchsurfing. Yet, what exactly defines such an authenticity in practice differed from person to person. While Rose searched for "local food", another interviewee, 33-year-old Wen, proudly related his "real Dutch experience" of attending a graduation ceremony and a family gathering:

> He [the host] asked me if I was interested in his friend's graduation ceremony. Of course I said yes! When can you get the chance to attend a Dutch graduation ceremony? [...] I went to the ceremony, and then I was invited to his friend's family gathering at the café near the university. [...] This kind of Dutch life can be experienced by neither joining a package tour nor being a backpacker; only couchsurfers have the chance to be involved in a Dutch family and experience the real local life.

Wen's identity as couchsurfer was not only defined by his physical mobility, but also involved a kind of connoisseurship of places, people and cultures (Szerszynski and Urry, 2002), to show an intellectual and aesthetic stance of "openness" and good taste for exploring the wider shores of authentic cultural experience (Regev, 2007). This identity was – at least partly – built in terms of a critique of mass-tourism (Cohen, 1988), reflecting an elitist view that "other people are tourists while I am a traveller" (MacCannell,

1999:107). Many Taiwanese couchsurfers claim that other tourists and backpackers are superficially "sightseeing", while they, by connecting to local people, can deeply understand local culture and experience "real local life". In this sense, the practice of couchsurfing and the experience and learning of cosmopolitan life not only require economic capital to travel around, but also cultural capital in form of the ability to "see through" the tourism myth and build a "real connection" with the culture of people and places.

In Taiwanese couchsurfing practice, as much as in Western forms of travel and tourism, the quest for the "authentic" is subject to a powerful, socially construed narrative or myth. It is formed and formulated in terms of culturally specific codes and aesthetic norms, and as much as these codes and norms do differ from one society to another, so do the claimed "authenticities" and their deceptions. A dialogue between 26-year-old Ho and 28-year-old White exemplifies these ambiguities. Both had been couchsurfing together, staying with a Korean family, and expected "typical Korean" cuisine and family life. Ho explained that in the morning the mother had made breakfast for them – very big sandwiches. Ho asked if they (the Korean family) normally had this for breakfast. The Korean mother responded that they normally did not eat sandwiches, but pickles. She had prepared the sandwiches especially for her guests, thinking that they were not used to Korean pickles. Ho said that at that moment she just shouted in her mind, "No, we are here for the local Korean food! Not sandwiches". White said that "we travel via couchsurfing because we really hope to experience the authentic local life, but these kinds of things sometimes happen, which is a surprise".

In fact, White's and Ho's expectation of experiencing "typical Korean dishes" is not dissimilar from that of a traditional tourist, the very attitude that most Taiwanese surfers want to get rid of. Similar to Culler's (1981:127) description of tourists as "the unsung armies of semioticians all over the world", Taiwanese surfers focus on signs of nation-based culture, such as "typical" Italian behaviour, exemplary Oriental scenes, typical American thruways, traditional English pubs, etc. (also see MacCannell, 1999:27). Such signs of nation-based culture constitute what Selwyn defines as "tourism myths" (Selwyn, 1996). While tourists collect such signs in their tourist resorts and sites of attractions, Taiwanese surfers collect them in their hosts' lives. In this sense, couchsurfing is still a type of tourism whose attractions are framed within the culture of the travellers, rather than those of their destinations (Haldrup and Larsen, 2010). Hosts, as part of their specific hospitality culture, may have different ideas about how their culture should be represented to foreign visitors, which in some cases leads to thwarted expectations, as in Ho's and White's Korean experience.

The contexts can become even more complex where signs of nation-based culture also travel and get remixed within realms of transnational social life. Ru, for instance, a 26-year-old female, told me the story of her stay with a Canadian host while in London. Ru's host loved exotic dishes, so they went to have Turkish and Ethiopian food. She explained that she felt "kind of weird" because what she had experienced was not English at all. "I was in England, but I was eating Turkish and Ethiopian dishes with a Canadian!" she explained. Yet, London is itself often described as a "world in one city", where many different kinds of people try to live together (Binnie et al., 2006:1). In this sense, the cultural medley Ru experienced actually is quite close to the reality of London. However, this type of "real local experience" seems not to have been the one she was looking for; what she expected was a "pure English cultural" experience. Whatever that may be, in any case it was not eating Turkish food with a Canadian. In this sense, the "local real" that Ru, White and Ho had been looking for was inscribed into their own cosmopolitan travel imagination, rather than in the grounds of their journey.

In brief, in the understanding of many Taiwanese surfers, hosts are expected to provide a taste of "pure local culture", while foreign surfers are expected to contribute to the exoticism of their "other culture" to their hosts' daily lives. Cosmopolitanism becomes a lifestyle that is strongly connected to the Taiwanese couchsurfers' narratives of personal belonging, which do not necessarily refer to an identity as global citizens. This lifestyle is built, on the one hand, upon displays of participation in modern life (where access and experience of "cultural diversity" is a major token), and on the other a sense of nostalgia embodied in the quest for the pure and real in local culture.

Learning stereotypes to "deal" with cultural difference

For many Taiwanese members, couchsurfing represents a means to learn cosmopolitan abilities, in particular knowledge about how to deal with "cultural difference". Stereotypes are a specific type of knowledge shared among many couchsurfers. According to Hilton and von Hippel (1996), stereotypes are a set of beliefs or opinions about characteristics, attributes and behaviours of members of certain social groups. In the cross-cultural interactions of couchsurfing, nation-based cultural stereotypes are to a large extent used to qualify people and their attitudes, tastes and values. Stereotypes about other cultures are among of the main knowledge-sources shared by couchsurfers in the process of learning to become a cosmopolite. In social psychology, stereotypes are considered important for the interplay of social interactions among different social groups. Stereotypes come as collective beliefs or group identities that allow group members to recognise one another, and represent the groups' characteristics (McGarty, Yzerbyt and Spears, 2004). In a global community such as couchsurfing, with people from different social and cultural backgrounds, nation-based cultural stereotypes often play a similar role in both online and offline interactions. In the case of the Taiwanese couchsurfers who were part of this study, such stereotypes work in a more complex way, mainly because cosmopolitan identity is also involved in the process by which the stereotypes affect how Taiwanese couchsurfers represent themselves, and how they understand and interact with others.

Hua, whose case has been mentioned above, explained how nation-based cultural stereotypes and cosmopolitan identity work hand in hand. In her interactions with couchsurfers from other countries, Hua was conscious of the dominant stereotypes associated with Taiwanese people, who are considered to be overly polite and punctilious. To be "more cosmopolite", she consciously conformed less to the stereotype of the Taiwanese. In this sense, stereotypes of other cultures are understood as part of cosmopolitan knowledge, while these stereotypes are used by couchsurfers to understand people from these cultures and to develop the skills to interact with them. Wen, whom I already mentioned above, provided an example. For him, the idea – or stereotype – that Germanic peoples are particularly conscientious influenced the way in which he addressed his potential Germanic hosts:

> I found that Western people, especially Germanics like Germans or Dutch, care about people's attitudes, and they are conscientious and careful. They do not appreciate when a person acts sensitively. So, before I travel to the Netherlands, I added as much information about myself in my profile as possible. I also uploaded many pictures of my daily life.

Taiwanese couchsurfers develop their cultural skills and cosmopolitan abilities based on such stereotyped knowledge of other cultures, which subsequently allows them to organise their own journey into and through other cultures. This is, of course, an observation not limited to Taiwanese couchsurfers, but also to other people's understanding of Taiwanese couchsurfers and how to interact with them. Ru related another experience she had in London:

> Before I went to her place, she sent me an email to complain about her last surfer from Hong Kong. She said, firstly the girl stayed in her living room and put her [the surfer's] stuff everywhere, as if she was in her own place. Secondly, when they went to a supermarket to buy stuff, the girl didn't say she would share the cost. The host thought she [the surfer] should pay at least half of the cost, because what they bought was food, which is supposed to be shared. She thought we were from the same culture, and she imputed such behaviours to Chinese culture. She said, 'I know the way you Chinese treat guests is different from us. In your culture, guests have to be made as comfortable as if they were at home. Guests need to do nothing but be served. However, our culture is not like this'. She even said, 'I can understand', but I know what she meant was, 'I cannot stand it'. She also said, 'your single-child-policy in China has spoiled your kids and made them not know how to respect others'.

Ru's British host grossly generalised in her preconceptions about Chinese culture, and also about a wider Asian world, including Hong Kong, Taiwan and China. The host stressed that "all the young people from Hong Kong, Taiwan and China are spoiled children", even though the single-child policy is never practiced in Hong Kong or Taiwan. Stereotypes are always prone to become prejudices, which are attitudes directed toward people because they are members of a specific social group (Brewer and Brown, 1998). Theoretically and ideally, stereotypes of other cultures should be challenged through the observation of, and interaction with, such cultures. The formation of stereotypes of a social group is a dynamic process in which the stereotype is shaped by the members of the inner group and people from other groups when they interact with each other (Berndsen, Spears, McGarty and van der Pligt, 1988). Nation-based cultural stereotypes are, in practice, not easily broken; more often they are repeated or even strengthened in the cross-cultural interactions between couchsurfers. When a couchsurfer behaves differently from the nation-based cultural stereotype, he or she might be seen as an exception, since he or she is thought of as a cosmopolitan couchsurfer. Cosmopolitan identity is used to explain the inconsistency between these stereotypes about other cultures and the behaviours of the couchsurfers from those cultures. As a result, the inaccuracy of such stereotypes cannot be reflected or revised in the cross-cultural interactions of couchsurfing. 29-year-old Jungle's stereotype of the Japanese illustrates this process:

> Japanese [...] is an ethnic [identity] with a closed mind. I think those Japanese who open their houses to surfers are freaks for most Japanese. Since they open their houses to surfers, they must be interested in foreigners or other cultures, I guess. I have some Japanese friends whom I met at university, and they are not interested in Taiwan or other countries at all. In the end I found that it was more interesting to talk with Japanese friends I met through couchsurfing. At least they are more friendly to other cultures.

Jungle's stereotype about Japanese people is that they are narrow-minded. When he meets several "open-minded" Japanese through couchsurfing who do not conform to the stereotype, he thinks that they must be seen as "freaks" by other, "typical" Japanese. According to McGarty, Yzerbyt and Spears (2004), a stereotype is changed when actual difference is observed. As Jungle's case shows, the contrary is the case. The stereotype of Japanese narrow-mindedness remained the same, even though the Japanese couchsurfers that he met were totally different from the Japanese stereotype in his mind.

In most cases, stereotypes are associated with an "imagined geography". For instance, in the West, Asia is often constructed as a mysterious, historical and exotic "Other" (Crang, 1998:66-69). In other words, the West has produced an "imagined Asia" and assigned Asian countries and people specific roles in the global cultural geography (Haldrup and Larsen, 2010). The stereotypes of Asian people held by many Western people are sometimes strengthened by Asians themselves. While the tourism industry in non-Western countries usually anticipates Western expectations with regard to local culture and other stereotypes (Hall and Tucker, 2004:6), a similar strategy is also adopted by some Taiwanese couchsurfers. For example, when Wen, conscious of Western expectations, chose gifts for his Western hosts he actually performed the stereotype of an imagined Asia so as to correspond to these expectations:

> They are Western people, so I suppose they like a gift in traditional Chinese style. I prepared a gift, a folding fan for my host in Groningen. I bought it at the Palace museum shop in the airport. The bone of the fan was made of wood. The cover of the fan was cloth with a flower-and-bird painting.

On the one hand, Western expectations lead Taiwanese couchsurfers to represent their culture in traditional or exotic ways. On the other hand, the traditional or exotic cultural images mobilised by Taiwanese couchsurfers strengthen stereotypes about Asians in the Western perspective (Chen, 2012). Therefore, stereotypes have little chance to be challenged or negotiated. This phenomenon of self-otherisation is more obvious when a Western host meets a non-Western surfer. Zhu, a 25-year-old female surfer, explained that it is the surfer's task to "please the hosts". She said that, "The best way to please the foreigner hosts is to tell them old traditions and customs about Taiwan. Mostly they are happy with that". Also she said, "To be honest, I don't really care if the information is true or not; the main point is to please the hosts, and this is the surfer's task". Zhu's words point toward an unequal relationship in couchsurfing, in which the host is a giver and the surfer is a receiver. Moreover, "to perform Taiwanese culture" in order to fulfil the host's expectations is the best way to please the host, according to Zhu. In this case, the unequal relationship between Western hosts and non-Western surfers strengthens a self-otherisation process, as well as affirming Asian stereotypes in the Western view.

Conclusion

The aim of this chapter has been to study how couchsurfing enables Taiwanese hosts and guests to experience, practice and learn the global ideology of "cosmopolitanism" at individual level. For most of the Taiwanese surfers who took part in this study, cosmopolitanism is less a transcendental philosophy of world citizenship than a complex set of knowledges about other countries or cultures, and a specific attitude prescribing how to deal with difference. The observation of individual interpretations and practices demonstrates that cosmopolitan perspectives are shaped in the interplay of collectively held stereotypes and personal expectations about the respective "Other". In some cases, this leads to an active challenging of cultural presumptions; in others, more often, it paradoxically has an opposite effect of reinforcing stereotypes and social exclusion. While for the Taiwanese couchsurfers cosmopolitanism defines, above all, an attitude of open-mindedness with regard to different nations and cultures, it is operated in practice through stereotypes categorising the world in terms of local entities differentiated by different "cultures". In this sense, cosmopolitanism allows one to participate in a global lifestyle, while at the same time it fuels a sense of nostalgia embodied in the quest for the pure or real at the local scale. Most Taiwanese couchsurfers claim that cosmopolitan knowledge can be learned through the repetition of cross-cultural interactions that take place within the context of couchsurfing. However, many stereotypes are not easily broken through couchsurfing, and some of the most excessive continue to be performed and shared among couchsurfers without much reflection. Therefore, disregarding its naive emphasis on equality, much couchsurfing practice unconsciously reproduces cultural biases and discriminations. For non-Western – such as Taiwanese – couchsurfers, self-transformations from parochial to cosmopolitan identities are therefore a complex and ambiguous process, in which nation-based cultural stereotypes and cosmopolitan identities both influence how surfers represent themselves, and how they interact with others. Many feel cosmopolitan as a result of having experienced different forms of travel, contact and mobility, yet at the same time they feel frustrated for being assigned a highly resilient role of "exotic other" in the contact zones with Western couchsurfers.

References

Beck, U. (2000) "The cosmopolitan perspective – on the sociology of the second age of modernity". *British Journal of Sociology* 51:79-106.

Beck, U. (2004) "The cosmopolitan turn". In N. Gane (ed.) *The future of social theory*. London: Continuum, pp.143-166.

Beck, U. (2006) *The cosmopolitan vision*. Cambridge: Polity.

Beck, U. (2011) "Cosmopolitan sociology: outline of a paradigm shift". In M. Rovisco and M. Nowicka (eds.) *The Ashgate research companion to cosmopolitanism*. Burlington, VT: Ashgate, pp.17-32.

Berndsen, M., Spears, R., van der Pligt, J. and McGarty, C. (1988) "Illusory correlation and stereotype formation: making sense of group differences and cognitive biases". In C. McGarty, V.Y. Yzerbyt and R. Spears (eds.) *Stereotypes as explanations: the formation of meaning beliefs about social groups.* Cambridge: Cambridge University Press, pp.90-110.

Binnie, J., Holloway, J., Millington S. and Young, C. (2006) "Introduction: grounding cosmopolitan urbanism: approaches, practice and policies". In J. Binnie, J.Holloway, S. Millington and C.Young (eds.) *Cosmopolitan urbanism.* New York: Routledge, pp.90-110.

Brewer, M.B. and Brown, R.J. (1998) "Intergroup relations". In D. T. Gilbert, S. T. Fiske and G. Lindzey (eds.) *Handbook of social psychology.* Fourth edition. Boston: McGraw-Hill, pp.554-594.

Chen, D.J. (2012) "Global concept, local practice: Taiwanese experience of couchsurfing". *Journal of Hospitality and Society* 1(3):279-297.

Cohen, E. (1988) "Traditions in the qualitative of sociology of tourism". *Annals of Tourism Research, Special Issue* 15: 29-46.

Crang, M. (1998) *Cultural geography.* London: Routledge.

Culler, J. (1981) "Semiotics of tourism". *American Journal of Semiotics* 1:127-140.

Dower, N. (2008) "Question the questioning of cosmopolitanism". In S.van Hooft and W. Vandekerckhove (eds.) *Questioning cosmopolitanism.* London: Springer, pp.3-20.

Germann Molz, J. (2007) "Cosmopolitans on the couch: mobile hospitality and the Internet". In J. Germann Molz and S. Gibson (eds.) *Mobilizing hospitality: the ethics of social relations in a mobile world.* Burlington, VT: Ashgate, pp.65-80.

Haldrup, M. and Larsen, J. (2010) *Tourism, performance and the everyday.* New York: Routledge.

Hall, C.M. and Tucker, H. (2004) "Tourism and postcolonialism: an introduction". In C.M. Hall and H. Tucker (eds.) *Tourism and postcolonialism: contested discourses, identities, and representations.* New York: Routledge, pp. 1-24.

Hannerz, U. (1990) "Cosmopolitans and locals in world culture". *Theory, Culture and Society* 7(2-3):237-51.

Hilton, J.L. and von Hippel, W. (1996) "Stereotypes". *Annual Review of Psychology* 47: 237-71.

MacCannell, D. (1999) *The tourist.* New York: Schocken.

McGarty, C., Yzerbyt, V.Y. and Spears, R. (2004) "Social, cultural and cognitive factors in stereotype formation". In C. McGarty, V.Y. Yzerbyt and R. Spears (eds.) *Stereotypes as explanations: the formation of meaning beliefs about social groups.* Cambridge: Cambridge, pp.1-15.

Kennedy, P. (2009) "The middle class cosmopolitan journey: the life trajectories and transnational affiliations of skilled EU migrants in Manchester". In M. Nowicka and M. Rovisco (eds.) *Cosmopolitanism in practice.* Burlington, VT: Ashgate, pp.19-36.

Nowicka M. and Rovisco, M. (2009) "Introduction: making sense of cosmopolitanism". In M. Nowicka and M. Rovisco (eds.) *Cosmopolitanism in practice.* Burlington, VT: Ashgate, pp.1-17.

Regev, M. (2007) "Cultural uniqueness and aesthetic cosmopolitanism". *European Journal of Social Theory* 2007(10):123-138.

Roudometof, V. (2005) "Transnationalism, cosmopolitanism and globalization". *Current Sociology* 2005(53):113-135.

Selwyn, T. (1996) *The tourist image: myths and myth making in tourism.* Hoboken, NJ: John Wiley & Sons.

Szerszynski, B. and Urry, J. (2002) "Cultures of cosmopolitanism". *Sociological Review* 50(4):461-481.

Urry, J. (2002) *The tourist gaze.* London: Sage.

Werbner, P. (2008) "The cosmopolitan encounter: social anthropology and the kindness of strangers". In P. Werbner (ed.) *Anthropology and the New Cosmopolitanism: rooted, feminist and vernacular perspectives.* Oxford: Berg, pp.47-68.

6. Allures of the Global, Gender and the Challenge to Confucian Hospitality among Vietnamese Couchsurfers from Ho Chi Minh City

Bernard Schéou

Introduction

While 60 % of the world population is concentrated in Asia, less than 10 % of the members of the global couchsurfing hospitality community live in Asian countries.[1] What are the factors that explain the apparently lesser "success" of this hospitality community among Asians? To respond to this question, I carried out an empirical case study in Vietnam. The focus was on the Vietnamese couchsurfers living in Ho Chi Minh City (HCMC), the first and largest city of the country, which accounts for 7 % of the Vietnamese population and 22 % of its urban population (General Statistics Office Of Vietnam, 2011). 51 % of all Vietnamese couchsurfing members live in HCMC. To collect data, I used several sources of information. I first built a database based on the profiles of the 689 couchsurfers living in HCMC. I selected the Vietnamese-speaking members only, in order to exclude Western expatriates (who only spoke English). I also excluded all incomplete and inactive profiles. Based on this initial information, I conducted interviews with Vietnamese couchsurfing members from HCMC. Because I was particularly interested in the challenges to hospitality within

1 | Cf. World Population Prospects, United Nations, 2011. All national statistics presented in the chapter about couchsurfing are from http://www.couchsurfing.org/statistics.html. Since the end of June 2012, statistics by country are no longer available on the website.

the context of private family homes, I sought to interview in particular those couchsurfers who were living with their families (according to the status they advertised on their profile pages).[2] I contacted 20 couchsurfers by email; only two did not respond. 13 agreed to be interviewed, and 11 interviews were eventually conducted. Of the 11, five were living with their families. I did the interviews in English, exploring a number of key issues: the decision to join the network, the activities engaged in, the experiences with other members (guests or not), the relationship between members and their families and neighbours, and the way the family was implicated in hosting (when appropriate). The interviews took place in the homes of the interviewees – for the ones who hosted – and in a coffee house for the others. The interview duration varied between 26 and 100 minutes, and led to 12 hours of recording – all of which have been transcribed.

COUCHSURFING AND THE ALLURE OF THE GLOBAL

In 1986, the communist state government of Vietnam decided on a series of political changes, which the Vietnamese call *đổi mới* (which can be translated as "renovation policy"). Until then, Vietnam's national history had been marked by a century of French colonisation, followed by 30 years of war (the Indochina War from 1946 to 1954, the Vietnam War from 1964 to 1975, the Cambodian-Vietnamese War from 1978 to1979 and the Sino-Vietnamese War in 1979). During this period, the South pursued a distinct destiny that continued during the Vietnam War, which was also a civil war between North and South. One of the first decisions taken by the victorious North in 1975 was the complete closure of the reunified country, and the forced collectivisation of the South two years later, resulting in a huge exodus of people fleeing abroad (Hitchcox, 1994; Khoa, 2004). The renovation policy initiated in the country in 1986 broke with the formerly rigid state control, and encouraged individual family initiatives as a means to achieve

2 | A "yes" means that a member is willing to accept couchsurfers to stay at his place; a "maybe" signifies that the member is not sure whether or not to host; a "not right now/but I can hang out" means that the member can't host couchsurfers but is ready to hang out with them; a "no" means that the member doesn't want to host or hang out; an "I'm travelling" indicates that the member is currently travelling.

the state's objectives of economic growth, national prosperity and integration within the international community (Phong, 2009). In 1988, the borders were opened to tourists, foreign investors and the Vietnamese diaspora. Today, the country is part of an area of strong economic growth, averaging around 6 % per year until 2012 (OECD, 2012). It has been observed that the Vietnamese – especially the youngest, who have known neither war nor the collectivist period – are fond of the consumption of branded products: clothes, cell-phones, netbooks, expensive jewellery, motorbikes and so on (Ashwill and Diep, 2005; Dovert and Lambert, 2004). Vietnam is changing quickly, becoming a consumer society where consumption is no longer solely a means to satisfy needs but, increasingly, a means of social differentiation (Benoit, 2011). In this new context it is difficult to comprehend the lives of the Vietnamese in terms of individual freedoms before the *đổi mới*. The government had by then established strict control over people's lives. It was difficult to communicate outside the country (mail was censored), and the Vietnamese were forbidden to talk to foreigners or to receive them at home; they were also prevented from studying abroad or even leaving the country (Luguern, 1997).

Today, the Internet's rate of penetration in Vietnam is 34 %, with over 30-million people online, compared to 26 % on average in other Asian countries, 79 % in North America and 61 % in Europe (Miniwatts Marketing Group, 2012). Facebook, which is censored, is used by millions of Vietnamese, who know how to circumvent the ban. Most Vietnamese, whether they live in Vietnam or abroad, are in contact with people from abroad, especially through the Internet. Couchsurfing represents one specific means to establish such contact with foreigners. The Vietnamese members of the network living in Ho Chi Minh City are relatively young (90 % are under 30 years old and 40 % are under 23), with a female majority (60 %). One third are students, whereas others are working persons, mainly working in office jobs in positions as diverse as director, manager, office assistant, seller, employee and secretary. More than half of them grew up in HCMC. 45 % have never travelled; 31 % have travelled only in Asia; 15 % have been to Europe and 10 % to America. The English language appears to be a primary condition for participating actively in the couchsurfing network. The proportion of those who are ready to host is low: only 14 % have "yes" as their couchsurfing status, and 27 % "maybe". In HCMC, among the Vietnamese members a few dozen are very active, mainly desiring to accommodate and meet other members, but much less participate as guests. Fewer than a hundred have low activity, while most others are inactive.

The interviewees who were part of my study were all couchsurfing members, even if not all were active hosts. Their decision to join was mainly influenced by a friend who was already a member. As Tran, a 24-year-old couchsurfer from HCMC, said: "I just [joined] because of Kate. [...] I saw that she can meet a lot of friends". Tran's friend, Kate, a 24-year-old who worked as sales administrator, joined because of a Vietnamese friend who travelled around Europe using couchsurfing, after spending one year studying in Spain: "She found in couchsurfing very good [people] and a very, very cool [community]", Kate explained. Phan, a 27-year-old man from Can Tho (Mekong Delta), joined the network because he saw a picture of one of his colleagues taken during a couchsurfing party: "I asked about it because I saw some foreigners there". The first time Thanh, a 22-year-old graduate student, heard about couchsurfing was when he read a message posted by a friend on Facebook. Hieu, a 24-year-old student, became aware of couchsurfing through a friend who had worked in the US for two months and told him about it. Long, a 28-year-old man who worked for a bank, joined the network following the recommendation of a colleague. The best friend of To, a 26-year-old man working in an industrial food company, was already a member, and one day she asked him to come with her to meet a Chinese couchsurfer, who asked To to host him. The three others learned about couchsurfing by reading articles in magazines or newspapers (Ha, Mai and Hieu).

The decision to join couchsurfing is usually carefully considered, and sometimes takes years. It involves being sure about what one is undertaking by reading the website carefully. A person needs to be ready to assume the role that he or she imagines he or she has to fulfil. For example, Ha, a 23-year-old student, waited two years to master the English language before joining: "two years ago I read [about it in] a newspaper. [...] I studied English and I studied at an international university, so I'm confident about my English – so I became a member of this website". Two years also passed between the moment when Kate heard of couchsurfing and when she joined. Why? She said she needed to think about the idea and to see how it was for her friend before making the leap. And it was even longer for Tran, who was told about couchsurfing four years before joining. Even now, neither of them is hosting.

There are many reasons that led my interviewees to join couchsurfing. One of the most commonly cited was to improve their English language abilities. Many couchsurfers explained that English is the language of business in the entire Asian continent, and that speaking fluent English is one of the conditions for finding a good job, preferably in a foreign company.

"Making friends before travelling" was another reason. The interviews showed that it is very important to know a future host to some degree before going into their home. Hosting or meeting people appear to be the best ways for someone who wants to travel through couchsurfing. This allows them not only to fill their address books, but also to learn about other people and cultures in order to be better prepared to travel. This was explicitly expressed by most of the interviewees. For example, couchsurfing was recommended to Hieu by a friend because he intended to travel after his studies: "he knew that [my intention was] to travel two years later, after my work was finished, so he introduced me [to couchsurfing] and said it would help me a lot [get] a lot of friends [...] and know about their cultures better". Tran said, "If I had the chance to go to their country, I would have some friends". Kate had the same idea: "I want to meet friends around the world because I will come [to visit them]". This familiarity reduces the anxiety which is generated by the idea of being hosted by strangers. Although she planned to extend a business trip in Thailand with a few days of couchsurfing, she confessed: "I'm a little bit worried, even scared".

"Meeting foreigners" can be a long-held dream. It can be linked to a curiosity about, and even a fascination for, strangers, and especially those from the West. For To, it dated back to his high-school days: "When I was in high-school, I travelled every day from here to downtown and back, and I saw a lot of foreigners and I hoped that one day I could talk to a foreigner. I could be friend with them and we could talk about anything". Phan had always been attracted to Western culture: "I liked Western culture when I was very young, so that's why I studied English when I was very young, but I don't know how to meet people. [...] I want to see their ideas. I want to see how they [have] fun and enjoy life, something like that". This attraction to Westerners was sometimes accompanied by a manifest indifference for other Vietnamese couchsurfers, who [could] consequently be offended – like Nga was, when she went to a couchsurfing meeting for the first time with a friend: "I sat at a table [...] with some Vietnamese people and very young girls, very young guys, and I talked to them, but they didn't listen to me; [they] listened to foreigners and they talked to foreigners, and I said to my friend, I don't like this party". Phan, who used to go to a lot of meetings each week, thought that some Vietnamese girls went to the gatherings because they wanted to meet foreigners in order to find a relationship, which he believed is not traditionally accepted in Vietnam. His feelings about this situation had changed, though: "Now I'm open-minded about that, but the first time I joined couchsurfing and I met some Vietnamese girls I felt [as though] they didn't like to meet Vietnamese couchsurfer guys like me. [...] Now I feel I'm ok with most of the girls I saw recently. Recently I see [that] many people who have a good education join couchsurfing, but before, the first time I went there, most of them were like prostitutes or people who work in a bar".

"Promoting Vietnamese culture" was another motivation that often came up in interviews. This was the prime reason given by Thanh: "I think I can give them advice [about things] I know about Vietnam; that's why I'm so excited about couchsurfing..."

"Meeting people, exchanging, learning from each other" could be considered a more cosmopolitan motivation, suggested by several interviewees. For Kate, couchsurfing was "like a bridge to make the people around the world [seem] like [they are] in the same country: the Earth". Tran explained: "because I like to meet people, I like to talk, I like to share, I like to know about them, and I even want to know people from many countries. Some I like, some I don't like... but when [I'm] talking to them I feel [that] I improve my knowledge".

"Finding opportunities to have fun" was not presented as a motivation as such. Nevertheless, it was a very immediate concern expressed in the responses of many interviewees. This was particularly true of those who belonged to the Saigon group and enjoyed going out. It helped them to make "friends" quickly, and gave them many opportunities to have fun with these friends in the several night-time events organised by couchsurfers.

Sometimes, a more personal motivation emerged from the interviews. One of the interviewees clearly stated that she was looking for her soulmate. She used couchsurfing as one possible way to find him: "I'm looking for a true friend [with whom] I can spend time – I can sit beside him with no need to talk about anything, but feel very warm inside. I would feel they love me as friend, and I feel like at home with my family".

Gender

The decision to host couchsurfers seems much easier for males, whether they live alone or with their families. Thanh didn't host, because he lived in a dwelling 20 m^2 with other people, but he always offered the couchsurfers he met the opportunity to visit his hometown. There, they could stay in his parents' house. In this way he received a Russian couple and a German girl, about whom he talked with great pride: "A Russian couple and a German girl... a German girl to my hometown!!!!" As soon as he could rent a private room, he said, he would host couchsurfers. Phan hosted a lot, but stopped and changed his status to "not now/hang out" because he said that he needed to rent his free room in order to earn some money, having been unemployed for longer than a year. He suspected that those couchsurfers who were looking for hosts had the sole motivation of "saving money"; he had doubts about their sincere wish to meet locals. But he was happy to realise that "many people" contacted him after he stopped hosting, and he "met some really nice people because [he] knew that they really [wanted] to meet locals".

Even if 82 % of the females in my database chose "any" as preferred gender (18 % chose "female"), and so were prepared to host males, I felt from the interviews that this issue could cause uneasiness. Maybe the reason Kate cited for not hosting was not the real one: "[At] 11 pm they close the gate [...] my apartment [is] very [awkward]". Nga, a 24-year-old woman working in an international company, and Mai, a 21-year-old student, lived with their families. The first said that she was doing what she wanted, and that her parents trusted her, and so she hosted either men or women. The second, however, did not host males, because this would require much more space in the house to ensure a sufficient degree of separation between her and her male guest. Similarly, despite having "maybe" as her couchsurfing status, Lam, a 30-year-old woman, a native of Hanoï, had never hosted. She suggested various reasons. One was the fear of not meeting the expectations of her potential guests, particularly as regarded the flat ("in France, there is a room for the guests so everything is already there, you have a bed, you have the sheets, the towels") or her way of living ("I am also afraid of not doing well, in fact it means that when I work, I come home late at night [...] maybe I feel like staying, you know, just staying home"). She had the idea that foreign travellers could not understand the local constraints: "I do not know if couchsurfers understand our life here in Vietnam". Despite the reasons she put forward, however, it seemed as though the social rules and the prying of her neighbours (and even that of her parents) that she had internalised, all played an important role in her reluctance to go forward (although she had lived in France for several years and travelled to several European countries, because she came from a traditional family, she seemed not to have freed herself from social and cultural norms). This was also reflected by her embarrassment when she admitted that it was mostly men who sent her couch requests: "There are a lot of men who ask me [...] because I put "any" you see – it is both men and women..." But at the same time, she didn't want to change her preferred gender from "any" to "female".

It is a fact that females are often contacted by men: on their pages, Kate and Tran only had references from males. They were prudent, reading the profiles of those who contacted them closely, but never refused to meet them. Kate verified "where they are from, how old they are, when they register, the pictures, and also very important are the references". She tried to learn about their characters by reading their page. Tran felt safe in her country and her city: "What will happen to me if I meet?" Phan didn't show excessive prudence when he was hosting. For him, it was not possible to rely on profiles – at the very least because some do not know how to fill them in, and because it is possible to lie. He said he accepted everyone, depending on his available space, and also gave them the keys of his house so that they could come and go freely.[3] Long did the same during the first month: "For the first month, I didn't choose, select the people; if [I were] available, I would accept them. [...] If I am busy or [away] I give the keys to my neighbours, [so that] the [visitors] can take them and get in". The second month, after finding that some people were looking for nothing else than free hosting, he began to select which requests he should accept, depending on how the request was written and whether or not the profile was fully filled out, including a photo.

For Ha, too, the profile had to be complete before he would accept a request. It was a condition for him to trust the person. Like Long, he was suspicious of those who "wanted free sleeping". If he didn't like the profile,

3 | Phan and Long are the only ones in my sample to give keys to their guests. When the couchsurfers live in the host's family, there is always someone home and the guests don't need keys. Only one host said he asked his guests to get out of the house: from seven to five, while he was at work (Hieu).

or if he had the feeling that they wouldn't "understand the Vietnamese culture" (as his family sometimes invited the couchsurfer for lunch or dinner), he refused to host.

Confucian knowledge and the challenges to hospitality

Besides the dramatic economic and societal changes that followed the political reforms of 1986, there is another element that is important to understand Vietnamese society today. Following Jamieson (1993), an American anthropologist, Vietnamese culture is a result of the intertwining, simplifying and Vietnamising of Taoist, Buddhist and Confucian influences over the centuries, although Confucianism (or more precisely Neo-Confucianism) was dominant in this process. The doctrine of Confucius aims to establish a harmonious society in which all members are bound together by mutual social obligations under a hierarchical framework, extending from the family to the nation: humans are primarily social beings who cannot act as if they are alone. This social framework, which relies on the family at base, is "focused on roles rather than on people, concerned with the welfare of the collectivity (family, village, nation) rather than with the feelings, desires, or problems of the individual" (Jamieson, 1993:19). This need for harmony in human relations conditions the behaviour of the individual, who must focus on fulfilling his or her role in society, paying attention to actions, words, gestures and feelings, and adapting to circumstances. The individual must be prudent and silent, rather than say something that might endanger harmony. He or she should strive to fade into the background by controlling feelings like anger, desire and sadness.

From this point of view, the practices of hospitality initiated by couchsurfing in Vietnam challenge the behavioural norms underlying the seemingly resilient Confucian heritage, especially with regard to two aspects. Firstly, the instruction to control emotions, resulting in a reserved attitude (Ngo, 2011), can make communicative exchanges difficult, given that the hospitality relationship is largely based on them, according to Bialski. She argues that, "in a hospitality exchange dyad, conversation is emotional because it is these emotions which become the language that the two have in common. Common human emotions which can be relayed through narratives, such as memories of pain, love, fear, or loss, are all common subjects among individuals, independent of their culture of origin" (Bialski, 2007:50). Secondly, couchsurfing hospitality practices contradict the "ancestral" advice not to disturb others by going into their homes (and its corollary, which is to not receive strangers). This comes, according to the anthropologist Khoa, from the fact that happiness relies on the fertility of the family group in the Confucian model, and implies a logic that "everyone has his own home [i.e. the family home]" (2009:23). Therefore, the study of hospitality practices appears to be a particularly useful way to better understand the changes in behaviours in Vietnam and, in particular, to examine the role played by the family in the changing social context of rapid modernisation in HCMC.

All my interviewees confirmed that hosting strangers at home was not a traditional Vietnamese practice. And when they said "stranger", they meant stranger to the family. According to Phan, "for most Vietnamese, they will think it's dangerous to let strangers into the house like me. [...] Hosting is not in the Vietnamese culture; we never let strangers into the house. [...] Maybe friends or relatives, but not strangers... the cousins it is ok but the cousin of the cousin, no". The friends to whom Long spoke about couchsurfing actually expressed fears for him and his property. Therefore, did the couchsurfers feel out of step with their families? This emerged clearly only in the responses of Kate and Phan (even if this does not mean that others did not sometimes feel the same).

Kate felt a deep divide between her and her family. She was troubled when she spoke about it. She was grateful to them for raising and feeding her, and because they paid for her studies at the university, but she did not feel happy when she was with them because of this gap, which she had difficulty in expressing it any other way than by saying, repeatedly, "we are different". And therefore she could share nothing with them; they could not talk together without arguing: "my parents are very... very... stubborn". Phan also reported a divide he felt from his parents. He lived in an apartment he owned, but which was chosen and mostly paid for (70 %) by his father: "they are of the older generation, so they want to buy a big place for my wife, for my children..." Without going into detail about the fissure between himself and his parents, he revealed that they did not share the same vision at all. He did not intend to get married and have children, but first wanted to travel, to move, to live elsewhere – especially in Western countries: "I think about that a lot, because now I have many things I want to do – I want to travel to this or that country, I want to see something. I don't know... I still want to move; I don't want to stay in one place. [...] It's really hard to say, but I meet some people... I don't know if someday, I will meet one girl and this will make me want to stop and don't want to move". He felt completely different from his parents: "I think 90 % different".

Those of my respondents who lived alone hid their involvement in couchsurfing from their families. Long told nothing about it to his parents: "I mean, they will worry a lot if strangers come in to share a room, so I think I should not tell them". Because he was hosting, his neighbours saw many foreigners in the building and thought that he was offering a kind of service for foreigners or tourists. He did not deny this. Phan had a brother and a sister, but he was the only one of his family to know about the network, "because we don't have too many conversations when we meet". His parents were always afraid of everything, and he did not like to worry them. If his father came into his home when he was hosting couchsurfers, he would simply say that they were friends. Friends: this is how the guests are usually presented by their hosts to their families or their neighbours. Even so, not all families readily welcome strangers, and the couchsurfer has to be convincing. Most of the time, couchsurfers use the argument that the system is good for them. For example, the first time that Ha invited a couchsurfer into his home, his mother did not appreciate it. But after he said that he wanted to improve his English and make friends from other countries, because he thought it would be beneficial in his future, she accepted it. He spoke of a student exchange-program: "I said that my friends came from Singapore and are just new there, and everybody believed that! Even my brother! When the neighbours saw me talk to foreigners, I said that they were friends from the university. So everybody thought that they were coming from the university as an exchange". Mai said that her mother was really open-minded and approved of her hosting girls from other countries, but when I discussed this with her mother I learnt that, in fact, she only agreed to host because she thought that this would help her daughter with her studies and help her get a career in international relations. This did not prevent her from giving a warm welcome to her daughter's guests, however.

In most cases, the family had confidence in their son's or daughter's choice of guest, and got used to having strangers in the home. Only one family was fully involved in the process, however: To's. When he received a request, he showed the picture to his family (especially to his mother), and they decided together if they would host or not. The whole family was very curious during the first hosting experience:

> they were excited and curious and when we... the Chinese guy and I... sat there and we had a conversation and we shared some, you know, like pictures and souvenirs; my family just sat there [...] so I told them I'm a member of a...it's really difficult to tell them about couchsurfing, so I just told them that I was a member of a website about cultural exchange and tourism and something like that. And when [foreigners] travel here, I introduce them to the culture and people and, if they want, they can stay with me to experience the local life...

He had always seen his family hosting strangers: "When I was a kid, I always saw my family host people: my relatives from the North, some people lived here for one or two years, they came from the North, so I think I [got] used to that, and my family [got] used to [having] different people in the house". But at the same time, To was scared that something could happen to his family while he was at work, even though he couldn't determine what it might be. He feared something, which could be as serious as paranoia about the behaviour of the guest or as simple as misunderstandings. This fear seemed to be fed by his inability to read the demeanour of foreigners: "because foreigners are so different... [with] Vietnamese we can guess by looking at the face, their behaviour...but [with] foreigners I have no idea, so they may have something in their mind something that they cannot show".

Expectations placed on the guests were few and relatively simple, but required that guests be attentive to local and individual habits and customs. The first expectation was that they should smile and be respectful, especially towards the elders. They should always inform their hosts by email before their arrival: "I'm living with my family and this is a household family with three generations, you meet a lot [of] people, so [to be] ready [to] smile and [show a] willingness to talk is better... I have to work [week-days] from 7am to 7pm, so during that time you have to take care of yourself of course and... my family, how to say, is selling food at the market, so we have to wake up early. [...] For the other things, they just watch me and follow [me], like [taking] off their shoes or something like that, it's quite easy". Ha helped them when they entered the house: "They show respect to the elder in the house, the family, because usually my grand-parents come here to watch the television, so when they enter the house and [meet them] they just smile or say hello, or say hello in Vietnamese... so the elders will think that they respect them. [Then] they are happy, and mum is happy with that". Two very important requirements in Ha's family were to keep the room clean and to open and lock the doors carefully: "Don't let them hear noise, it's easy". It may be easy to do, he said, but it's also easy to forget if you find it unimportant.

In addition, when I asked if they had had bad experiences, most respondents reported "anecdotal difficulties" in relation to lack of compliance with these (sometimes implicit) rules. And even if the rules might seem trivial, they were not thought of this way by the hosts. Here are some examples. Hieu's aunt was offended that a guest, after cleaning the room, gave her the trash to throw out because she did not know where to put it. Hieu thought that she should have done it herself, even though he admitted that he understood her situation. Ha seemed to be really affected by the issue of cleanliness: "One time, I hosted three people. [...] They really didn't keep [the] house clean, so that [made] my mum angry with me, so I think this was a bad experience". Long preferred to receive European people, because once, Asian couchsurfers left garbage in the room, and he had to clean it up. It's not really possible to say whether these three difficulties came from cross-cultural reasons, or arose from a lack of politeness. Problems might include a guest who does not come, even if he has confirmed his arrival, or another who comes back at 3am and awakens the parents, demanding that the door be opened. One cross-cultural difficulty that I have been told about does stem from traditional beliefs. Ha's mother refused a couple of guests entry into the house during the first days of the Tet, because to do so could bring bad luck to the house if they were to have sex during their stay. Another came from the reaction of a couchsurfer to the way his host was addressing him: "I felt he [was] like my little brother, so I called him kid. It's normal in Vietnam, [but] he didn't agree with that, so he told me 'you always [call] me [a] kid, I'm not [a] kid anymore – even my father and my brother [are] older than you, but they never call me [a] kid', and that made me feel me very bad". It was impossible for the couchsurfer to understand this custom, who had no idea that this way of addressing people is a traditional custom in Vietnam (Jackson, 1987). It is also probable that many cross-cultural misunderstandings occur, but were difficult to uncover. First, to do so would require that the interviewees talk about it. If they did not, it may be because these misunderstandings are more difficult to express during an interview, as they are related to more personal and deep-rooted feelings, especially as Confucian morality prevents the expression of emotions. Second, to recognise such misunderstandings requires a thorough understanding of the cultures of origin of both persons. Jamieson, who speaks Vietnamese and stayed many years in Vietnam, says of his experiences of and exchanges with the Vietnamese that "the number and scope of misunderstandings were incredible" (1993:ix).

Yet, all interviewees were conscious of differences between Westerners and Asian people. We saw earlier that Long preferred to receive Europeans. In contrast, To thought that it was easier to get along with Asian couchsurfers: "With Asians we [are] quite close in terms of culture, and it's easier than [with] Europeans or Americans". Phan found differences between Asians and Westerners when he was looking for a couch, and sent requests to locals and expatriates: "People from the West are easy to accept; they're very easy-going, they say ok, they just say, ok, let's come or something. But if I request Philippinos, Malaysians or something, they ask a lot of questions...what kind of people are you or something like that. [...] I think Asian people worry about the people they will let into their house, like Vietnamese [do]".

Conclusion

What surprised me most in the course of this study was the apparent prudence that characterised the behaviour of almost all Vietnamese couchsurfers interviewed. The way they joined the network was the first sign here. Most often, it followed a recommendation by a friend, and sometimes came only after years of careful consideration. Caution was also seen in the will to be prepared for events that might occur, and through actions put in place to avoid any surprises. This is the case when someone learns English for two years before joining the network in order to be ready to communicate. Caution was also shown by those who described, in great detail, the conditions of hosting on their profile. This was also the case for all those who received couchsurfers in order to (potentially) visit those they have hosted. This preparation therefore focused them on the role they would have to play in the relationship of hospitality.

Here, I risk an explanatory hypothesis to these attitudes. Whilst not wishing to ascribe too much importance to cultural explanations, can't all this be connected to the traditional emphasis put on the role of each person in the Vietnamese social system? What happens when this social system is challenged and eventually modified through receiving a stranger at home, or when someone escapes the system by travelling or by moving to Saigon? To be free from this system can be thrilling, but also a worry, and it is therefore not surprising that preparing properly for this new role is so important. How to act according one's desires, if this is against the social system and the family? After all, the opening up and modernisation of the country is relatively recent (even if this finding has to be put in perspective concerning the South, which has always been characterised by greater openness to the world, a greater degree of modernisation and more tolerance for individual initiative, according to many scholars) (Jamieson, 1993; Tertrais, 2004).

According to Tran (2010), the renovation policy allowed the expression of concerns previously stifled, like awareness of self and individual development. Therefore, he reports the growing importance of expressing emotions in Vietnam today, but it is difficult to say whether couchsurfers are more emotional from the interviews. Only one claimed to be very emotional, and demonstrated it very clearly during the interview in his attitude and his words. For the rest, there were very few who showed or reported their feelings during the interviews, although different emotions such as jealousy, admiration and sorrow were apparent at certain times.

Related to the fact that hosting or couchsurfing are contrary to tradition, I observed different attitudes within my small sample. All but one hid the existence of the network from their families, and more or less lied by presenting the couchsurfers as friends to their families. I do not know if their families were dupes or not, but those who are hosting now were not at all easy to convince the first time. For those who live alone there has, predictably, been no confrontation with the family. But girls, because they seem to have internalised traditional ways more completely, do not host even if they are living in Saigon and their families in Hanoi.

The two members of my sample who felt a deep divide from their families lived alone, but they were not hosting. It seems that they were both in search of a form of "happiness" and self-realisation. For them, this research exposed a life full of events and parties with other couchsurfers, and a different way of life from their parents. For both these interviewees, it appeared that couchsurfing filled an existing need, rather than having been the trigger for it. Phan felt that he was far from what he called the Vietnamese culture: "Now I'm in between. Not Vietnamese but not [a] Westerner [...] so I need to balance". In his case, there was clearly a gap between tradition, which he associated with his parents, and modernity, which he associated with the West. He wanted to (and could) have fun with young people worldwide through couchsurfing. Those who participated in the local group, and in organised events and parties, seem to have been more likely to be influenced by cosmopolitan values than those who merely hosted, especially when they still lived with their families. The family appeared most often as a bulwark, protecting the son or daughter from external influences. Being willing to receive strangers allowed families to satisfy the request of the son or the daughter (and could even help their children's careers), while controlling the situation and assimilating such influences without getting lost in them. So, even if it is an entirely new practice, to host within the family can, paradoxically, be a sign of the person's anchoring in Vietnamese culture, rather than a rejection of tradition. According to what the interviewees said, and the feelings I had in their houses, familial cohesion never seemed threatened by welcoming strangers but, rather, strengthened by it. This does not mean that there is no evolution under the influence of the foreigners, but the changes are controlled by the family, which "produces and innovates".

REFERENCES

Ashwill, M. and Diep, T.N. (2005) *Vietnam today: a guide to a nation at a crossroads*. Boston: Intercultural Press.

Benoit, H.D. (2011) *Le Viêt Nam*. Paris: Le Cavalier Bleu.

Bialski, P. (2007) *Intimate tourism, friendships in a state of mobility – the case of the online hospitality network*. Unpublished master's thesis, University of Warsaw, Warsaw.

Dovert, S. and Lambert, P. (2004) "La relation Nord-Sud. La clé de la construction nationale vietnamienne". In S. Dovert and B. d. Tréglodé (eds.) *Viêt-Nam contemporain*. Paris: Les Indes savantes, pp.31-115.

General Statistics Office of Vietnam (2011) *Statistical data about population and employment*. http://www.gso.gov.vn/default_en.aspx?tabid=467&idmid=3 (accessed 26 Sept 2012).

Hitchcox, L. (1994) "Relocation in Vietnam and outmigration: the ideological and economic context". In J.M. Brown and R. Foot (eds.) *Migration, the Asian experience*. London: MacMillan, pp.202-220.

Jackson, M.H. (1987) "Vietnamese social relationships: hierarchy, structure, intimacy and equality". *Interculture* 20(94):2-17.

Jamieson, N.L. (1993) *Understanding Vietnam*. Berkeley, CA: University of California Press.

Khoa, L.H. (2004) "Vietnamiens d'outre-mer? Communauté réelle ou diaspora potentielle". In S. Dovert and B. d. Tréglodé (eds.) *Viêt-Nam contemporain*. Paris: Les Indes savantes, pp.433-454.

Khoa, L.H. (2009) *Anthropologie du Vietnam. L'espace mental du lien*. Vol. 1. Paris: Les Indes Savantes.

Luguern, J. (1997) *Le Viêt-nam*. Paris: Karthala.

Miniwatts Marketing Group (2012) *Internet world stats*. http://www.Internetworldstats.com/stats.htm (accessed 28 Sept 2012).

Ngo, T.T.H. (2011) *Argumentation et didactique du Français langue étrangère pour un public vietnamien*. Unpublished PhD dissertation, Université Lumière Lyon 2, Lyon.

OECD (2012) *Southeast Asian economic outlook 2011/12*. OECD Publishing.

Phong, D. (2009) "Vietnam au XXe siècle, du Duy Tân au Doi Moi". In G. d. Gantès and N.P. Ngoc (eds.) *Vietnam. Le moment moderniste*. Aix-en-Provence: Publications de l'Université de Provence, pp.265-270.

Tertrais, H. (2004) "L'identité nationale vietnamienne". In S. Dovert and B. d. Tréglodé (eds.) *Viêt-Nam contemporain*. Paris: Les Indes Savantes, pp.19-29.

Tran, A. (2010) "The political economy of emotions & emotionality in post-reform Ho Chi Minh City". *SEAP E-Bulletin*, 11-17.

7. Cosmopolitanism as Subcultural Capital: Trust, Performance and Taboo at Couchsurfing.org

Jun-E Tan

Introduction

The phenomenon of trust in couchsurfing has piqued the interest of many researchers, resulting in a number of studies discussing reasons why and how trust happens within this specific social context. Bialski and Batorski (2009) suggest that it is the website's affordances that allow users to achieve a level of familiarity and make their trusting decisions based on homophilous characteristics. Trust is further enhanced when couchsurfers meet each other offline in a meaningful, private space that catalyses trust-building processes (Bialski, 2007). Other researchers have looked at the community as a possible explanation, explaining trust with the provision of a sense of belonging in the community and increased participation in it (Rosen et al., 2011), or the idea of the social network being a risk-mitigator (Tran, 2009). While these insights are important, there is no unified view on how trust works in couchsurfing, perhaps because of the complexity of this online community. Trust is multidimensional, involving individuals, the website, the community and the larger world beyond the couchsurfing community. To compound matters, more often than not researchers do not break down the concept of trust sufficiently to aid systematic analysis. The objective of this chapter is to study processes of trust-building at the hospitality community site Couchsurfing.org, in order to advance understanding of how, at a macro-level, an environment conducive to building trust is formed by an online community. Through describing social taboos on Couchsurfing and how the community members learn and accumulate subcultural capital, I arrive at the conclusion that it is through strategic impression management, according to certain socially desirable principles inscribed in the global ideology of cosmopolitanism, that a strong foundation for trust is built. I approach the question of how trust is built with a macro-level perspective of couchsurfing and a theoretical emphasis on trust. As argued by Coleman (1990:175), a macro-level view on a phenomenon of trust is useful because one looks at three components at a same time: the purposive actions of individual actors in placing or withdrawing trust; the micro-to-macro transition of individual trust to a system level; and then a macro-to-micro transition of the system-level trust back to the actions of the individuals in placing trust or being trustworthy.

The data-collection for my research was an extensive process spanning three years (from mid-2009 to mid-2012), which involved an immersion in the field, both online and offline. During periods of face-to-face data collection, I conducted participant observation both as a host and a travelling couchsurfer, and interviewed my guests and surfers, as well as other couchsurfers that I met along the way. In the pilot study from November 2009 to January 2010, I hosted 15 couchsurfers (from Singapore, Indonesia, Taiwan, Switzerland, Slovakia, Estonia, Germany, Poland, USA, Brazil, Nigeria and Australia) in my living room in Singapore, and interviewed them. A year later (April-August 2011), I conducted 21 interviews with my hosts and some couchsurfing volunteers while couchsurfing in some cities in the UK, France, Austria and the Netherlands. Participant observation was also conducted in Vienna during the Vienna Calling 2011, an annual couchsurfing event attended by more than 500 couchsurfers. Sampling was done with the intention of coming up with a diversified sample (in terms of demographics, e.g. age, gender, nationality, etc.), and snowball sampling was used to get access to potentially interesting members, such as active volunteers or ambassadors. In October 2011, I attended a conference in Berlin hosted by Couchsurfing International, and interviewed Casey Fenton, one of the co-founders of the organisation. During the intervals between "formal" data collection, I continued to host and couchsurf when I travelled.

By the time of this writing, I have been a host 50 times (56 individuals from 26 different nationalities) and surfed 28 times (23 locations across 10 countries in Europe, North America, Asia and Oceania). Most of the data drawn upon in this study are from the second phase of study (interviewing couchsurfing hosts), though some of the observations were made during the overall immersion in the field. For all of the interviews, respondents were given an informed-consent form to set out their rights as research subjects, explain issues of anonymity and the handling of data, and state their freedom to terminate the interview if they felt uncomfortable. All the names in this chapter have been changed to protect the anonymity of the subjects, with some demographic information furnished to provide some context.

TRUST IN COUCHSURFING

As argued in an earlier paper (Tan, 2010), I have found Möllering's theoretical framework (2006) useful to understand trust within Couchsurfing.org. Möllering defines trust as "an ongoing process of building on reason, routine and reflexivity, suspending irreducible social vulnerability and uncertainty as if they were favourably resolved, and maintaining thereby a state of favourable expectation towards the actions and intentions of more or less specific others" (Möllering, 2006:111).

Unpacking the concepts within the definition of trust according to Möllering, there are three bases of trust, namely reason, routine and reflexivity. These are common theoretical perspectives taken by researchers when studying trust. Reason is the rationalist paradigm that suggests that people trust by judging the trustworthiness of the other party. Routine is the "taken-for-grantedness" of trust, its source being presumably reliable institutions. The reflexivity approach taken by some researchers adopts a process view of trust-building, where actors work together to build trust gradually. Möllering explains that although trust literature in these branches attempt to explain trust, there is a danger that they may explain trust away. For example, if trust is purely based on reason and rational choice, the resulting lack of uncertainty would render the element of trust superfluous or trivial. If trust is something that is taken for granted, based on existing institutions, where did that trust come from? And thirdly, if trust is an ongoing, reflexive process through which trust is eventually built, the element of certainty that trust will be built would also render the idea of trust redundant.

The element that is missing in the picture, as argued by Möllering, is the concept of "suspension", which he also refers to as "the leap of faith":

> 'Suspension' is the process that enables actors to deal with irreducible uncertainty and vulnerability. Suspension is the essence of trust, because trust as a state of positive expectation of others can only be reached when reason, routine and reflexivity are combined with suspension (Möllering, 2006:110).

It is suspension that links reason, routine and reflexivity to trust; and trust thrives in an environment where there is irreducible uncertainty and vulnerability. Möllering suggests that the analogy of the leap of faith is useful to study how actors make the leap across the gap of the unknown. Trust-building will never be able to eliminate that gap altogether, because risk is a key condition for trust to exist – we should look instead at how the leap can be facilitated. For this, Möllering suggests some ways that actors use to suspend the uncertainty. One of the methods described (that is relevant to this study) suggests that the trustor and trustee work together to create a narrative in the trustor's mind, to enable him to trust. The trustee supplies the trustor with information that is used by the trustor to form a narrative about her trustworthiness. For example, the trustor reads the trustee's couchsurfing profile and forms a story about her background and the potential interaction between them. As information asymmetry is usually the case, the trustor needs the narrative to trust as if the unknown was known. To look at trust-building via the couchsurfing platform, we should then observe how users utilise the platform to create narratives of trustworthiness.

In the case of couchsurfing, looking only at the host end of the dyad, for simplicity's sake, I have found different layers of positive expectations when hosting a couchsurfer. Broadly put, the host expects that: 1) she will not be harmed, physically or in other ways such as being taken advantage of; 2) the guest is a pleasant person and is easy to get along with; and 3) it will be an interesting and fruitful cultural exchange. These layers are common themes provided by respondents when they elaborate on what their trust is in relation to. Different hosts have different levels of expectations, though most agree on expecting a safe interaction at the very least. Interestingly enough, many take safety for granted within the context of couchsurfing, and do not consider bodily harm or damage of property to be a probable scenario. Some emphasise that they want to interact with someone whom they feel comfortable with as a justification for the tendency to accept a guest they are similar to and would presumably get along with, whereas some do not care. As expressed by Laura, a 20-year-old host whose family welcomes surfers, "Maybe we will click and maybe we just – coexist.

Coexisting is fine with me". For those who expect more out of the interaction, their filtering process tends to be more stringent and thorough.

The complexity of the situation is heightened by the different backgrounds of the respondents, and also their perception of risk. Contrast a single man in his twenties living in a shared flat with a single mother living with a child – they have very different considerations where risk is concerned. As trust hinges upon perception of risk as a starting point, it is important to understand that risk is dynamic, contextual and historical (Tulloch and Lupton, 2003). I do not imply that simple causal connections between possible enablers of trust are indicators of trustworthiness and trust outcomes. This is consistent with the philosophy that trust is interpretative and contextual, subject to individual idiosyncrasies and experiences. Users are given the structural conditions and tools to support their trust, hence making it easier for them to make the leap of faith. However, a deterministic activation of trust based on these conditions is not implied.

PERFORMING COSMOPOLITANISM AS SUBCULTURAL CAPITAL

Although communications between couchsurfers and within the community can be broadly categorised into online and offline, all such communications emerge within the same social plane. As members of an online community (which in some cases leads to offline meetings and gatherings), couchsurfers are socialised into having a set of socially accepted values, attitudes and behaviours. This happens against a backdrop of globalisation and a world that is shrinking due to higher mobility of its citizens. A useful way to theorise this socialisation process is in terms of an accumulation of subcultural capital formed around a normative type of a cosmopolitan way of life.

Sarah Thornton, in her study of club cultures in the UK, draws upon Bourdieu's conception of cultural capital and applies it to subcultures (Thornton, 1996). The concept of cultural capital has been very useful for social scientists in areas of the maintenance of social stratification systems, social reproduction and mobility, while taking into account structural constraints and human agency (Lamont and Lareau, 1988). Lamont and Lareau (1988:156), in a widely cited paper, sieve through the work of Bourdieu and Passeron, and define cultural capital as "*institutionalised, i.e. widely shared, high status cultural signals (attitudes, preferences, formal knowledge, behaviours, goods and credentials) used for social and cultural exclusion*, the former referring to exclusion from jobs and resources, and the latter, to exclusion from high status groups" (original emphasis). In other words, people who own cultural capital are able to attain higher status in society. Research on cultural capital has focused very much on education (Lareau and Weininger, 2003) and is often linked to "high" culture, or cultural knowledge of the upper classes (Robson, 2009).

Thornton's notion of subcultural capital agrees with Bourdieu's view of cultural capital in social mobility through purposeful display of appropriate cultural signals, but removes the idea of class – and thus the debate on one class dominating another – and distances the concept from classic capital theory. Using the idea of cultural capital, but discarding the undertones of class and high culture, Thornton (1996) looks at subcultures and how the actors perceive and conceive "hipness" in objectified and embodied subcultural capital. One is considered to be cool if in possession of certain rare objects such as limited edition records, or is able to use appropriate slang.

Actors that own subcultural capital enjoy status "in the eyes of the relevant beholder" (Thornton, 1996:11). Although the concept of subcultural capital originated from the observation of club cultures in the UK, it has been used in a variety of other contexts, such as on underclass culture in Australia (Bullen and Kenway, 2005), underprivileged young men in Denmark (Jensen, 2006), Tikyan street boys in Indonesia (Beazley, 2003), young and wealthy "Stockholm Brats" in Sweden (Ostberg, 2007), spectator identity in world football (Giulianotti, 2002), etc. In applying Thornton's notion of subcultural capital, researchers exercise discretion and not all apply the distinctions that she identifies. There are, however, some commonalities among these studies.

Firstly, the concept is deployed within subcultures, which can be defined as "groups of people that are in some way represented as non-normative and/or marginal through their particular interests and practices, through what they are, what they do and where they do it" (Gelder, 2005:1). Secondly, research is done to see how, within an alternative space and hierarchical order, actors are able to gain status by amassing knowhow and attitudes prized within that space. Thirdly, studies that use the conceptual framework of subcultural capital usually identify an underlying trait that is important to the community, be it "hipness" (Thornton, 1996), "expressive masculinity" (Jensen, 2006), "toughness" (Bullen and Kenway), "stylishness" (Ostberg, 2007) or something else. This underlying trait may present different manifestations, but provides a basic foundation from which the members of the community will carve their behaviour.

What is the underlying trait of subcultural capital in the community of couchsurfers? As will be demonstrated and elaborated upon later, in the examination of social taboos in couchsurfing, it is the trait of cosmopolitanism that defines one's presentation of self in the community. There are multiple definitions of cosmopolitanism. One that is succinct and thought-provoking is that of Beck (2003:17), defining cosmopolitanism as a condition in which the "otherness of the other is included in one's own self-identity and self-definition". To break down the concept of cosmopolitanism, Kendall, Woodward and Skrbis (2009) draw upon Swidler's work on cultural repertoire (2003) and see cosmopolitanism as a "toolkit of habits, skills and styles from which people develop strategies of action". They suggest that different situations will induce different levels of the enactment of being cosmopolitan – cosmopolitanism is more than a disposition, it is a "*disposition performed*" (Kendall et al., 2009:107, original emphasis). Cosmopolitanism is therefore "a set of ideas, frame for interpretation, behavioural patterns, and knowledges that allow an individual to perform a cosmopolitan subjectivity" (ibid.:108), based on broad tenets of mobilities, cultural-symbolic competencies, inclusivity and openness.

Kendall et al. (2009) go on to suggest that there are two forms of cosmopolitanism: one that is banal and unreflexive, and based mostly on uncritical consumption of the Other; and another that is authentic and reflexive, where the cosmopolite is genuinely interested in and open to other cultures. The consumption of food, tourism, media and other products that result from a globalised situation in the *unreflexive* cosmopolite may result in cultural openness in intellectual and aesthetic domains; however, the *reflexive* cosmopolite has deeper emotional and ethical commitments. The reflexive cosmopolite empathises with and is interested in other cultures, and holds universalist values and ideas (with an orientation towards selflessness, worldliness and communitarianism) that are expected to reach beyond the local (Bauböck 2002:112, cf. Kendall et al., 2009).

Theoretically, it is possible to form a juxtaposition of the concepts of cosmopolitanism and subcultural capital in order to suggest that couchsurfers strategize their actions and behaviour according to cosmopolitan ideals that are prized within the community, and gain status and social acceptance through relevant presentation of self. The categorisation of reflexive and unreflexive cosmopolitanism by Kendall et al. is useful, because it is found in the data that being cosmopolitan is an important trait to couchsurfers, although not in all forms. As will be shown later, reflexive cosmopolitanism, with its emotional and ethical commitments as well as cultural sensitivities, forms the core trait of subcultural capital within the couchsurfing community.

For Germann Molz (2007), couchsurfing itself (or rather, hospitality exchange networks in general, but I shall focus on Couchsurfing.org in this discussion) is not an inclusive community by default. From here emerges a paradox: hospitality exchange networks that fundamentally reflect and advocate a cosmopolitan openness to difference actually delineate the "right" kind of difference from the "wrong". The former assumes that participants are middle-class and above, and have the means to travel and the ability to reciprocate in kind, with broader commonalities of interests in travelling and learning about other cultures. The latter, however, includes those who are in danger of turning from a "guest" to a "parasite", and whose difference "threatens rather than serves the cosmopolitan fantasy" (ibid.:77). The community is governed by reputation systems and other mechanisms that create the social structure, internalising this philosophy within the community.

Following Germann Molz, the community of couchsurfing is conditionally open to citizens of the world based on certain value judgements. However, I believe that the judgements run deeper than fears of attracting abusers of free hospitality – the situation hinges very much on the type of cosmopolitan attitude that is important for couchsurfers. My data show that the normative ideals of the couchsurfing community push for reflexive cosmopolitanism: a way of life that celebrates diversity and different cultures. For many, this is an ideological notion that is deeply emotional and connected to their sense of identity. This can be linked to the observation of a lament often heard amongst couchsurfers that they are not "typical" of members of their society – whom they deem narrow-minded, conservative people who often hold prejudices against people that are different. Sally, a single mother from Austria, explained why she hosts couchsurfers:

> I think it's, for me, one of the most important points to be open-minded, and to communicate with open-minded people, because I see a lot of racism, prejudice. I meet a lot of people, especially in my village, they are not at all open-minded and they are racist. And this is one of the worst things for me. To be tolerant is really important, I want to educate my son like this, and also, this is a point for me

that my son, through CS, has the chance to make experiences with open-minded people. And not to ask for colour of your skin, your income, your parents have a big car or whatever.

Another respondent, a 30-year-old man from Nigeria who surfed my couch, described the reflexive cosmopolitanism that is perceived of couchsurfers, and his appreciation of the cosmopolitan company:

I think there is this ethos and creed. A lot of people who do couchsurfing are very ethical. It is not specifically stated, but a lot of people feel that this is a system that makes the world a better place. [...] I feel that people are not looking at the destructive. They just want to make an impact. They just want to meet people, let them know about their culture, be an ambassador, network, I mean, just get to learn about the global village that the world is becoming now. I have never sat down with a Taiwanese and talked about world politics. I mean, that was a profound experience that would have never happened if I didn't surf.

Social taboos and norms of couchsurfing

In her study, Thornton states that while clubbers find it difficult to classify or describe their group, they are generally happy to identify a homogeneous crowd to which they don't belong, i.e. the mainstream – the opposite of hipness and sophistication. Taking a leaf out of Thornton's book, I look at social taboos on couchsurfing to discover attitudes and behaviours that are not appreciated in the community, and which may lead to social exclusion. Through this, we can see the underlying values and moral judgements commonly held by couchsurfers, and link the empirical situation with theory.

Through talking to couchsurfers in interviews or during informal interactions, I was able to observe that certain behaviours or attitudes are frowned upon by the majority of the members within CS. The worst taboo is arguably racism or other forms of prejudice, as this is the epitome of narrow-mindedness, and "not what couchsurfing is about". As put by Alina, a female host from Vienna in her twenties:

If I ever hosted somebody who would go on about - against stuff that I'm very much for, like against people of a certain skin colour, or against gays, or against people of a certain religion, I would certainly leave a negative reference, stating that, you know, 'it's couchsurfing, you should be open to everybody'.

From the point of view of some hosts, it is important that the surfer be more interested in the cultural exchange than the prospect of free accommodation. As explained by Sally, the single mother cited above: "I prefer to hear the reason why you request my couch, this is not because you have your own guest room, a big guest room with shower, but because you want to communicate with me. Or you like my area, you read my profile, and you think it could match". Money is taboo as well, or, specifically, using couchsurfing for commercial gain. When I bring up the idea of a "couchsurfing tip jar" (where the guest contributes some money to the host) in conversations, most couchsurfers expressed disapproval. Another oft-heard quote is, "couchsurfing is not a dating site", though sometimes this is expressed with a tinge of sarcasm. Using couchsurfing as a platform to have romantic encounters belittles its mission of creating "pure" intercultural relationships that rise above the banality of casual sex. In sum, it is not in the "couchsurfing spirit" to use the system with ulterior motives, and many couchsurfers believe strongly that it should be used for higher ideals, such as making the world a better place through a process of experiential learning about other cultures.

How do couchsurfers make judgements on people whom they have never met before? Requests that are copy-and-pasted or not personalised do not fare well, as they imply that the surfer is more interested in free accommodation than cultural exchange, which in turn is based on the premise that the surfer wants to meet the host for specific reasons (e.g. they share the same interests, they live in a very interesting part of town, etc.). References on the profile are important indicators that the owner has interacted with people from different cultures, and has no difficulties in getting along with them. Subtle cues on profiles can also serve as red flags. For instance, the "ethnicity" field has been met with some controversy,[1] and some respondents have stated that if someone fills in the ethnicity field with "white", this is a put-off, and will damage the person's chance of being accepted as a guest. An example is the following quote from Paul, a German host in his forties:

1 | See the discussion at http://wiki.couchsurfing.org/en/Ethnicity

As I said, if the person thinks that 'white' is an ethnicity that he needs to put forward, that tells me that either the person hasn't thought a whole lot, he's not a very intelligent person, or he's a racist. Because if you put that forward as your ethnicity, he thinks that... underlying I assume that the person thinks that being white is somehow superior to some other things.

Another commonly expressed example of a red flag is that of a male host stating his preference for hosting female surfers. "It's a really bad sign", said Mary, an Irish female couchsurfer in her thirties. This gives off an impression that the host is interested in hook-ups as a primary motivation for hosting, which is again, "not what couchsurfing is about".

While the value judgements and informal rules attempt to construct a cosmopolitan world where people are culturally competent, genuinely receptive to foreign cultures without ulterior motives and shun common prejudices and bigotry, it is also apparent that things are not as ideal in practice. A major allure for travelling through couchsurfing is the free accommodation offered, as many travellers are attracted by this aspect, and start off by surfing couches. A common narrative is that the new couchsurfer is enticed by the cheap way of travelling, but realises the additional benefits of meaningful cultural exchange after having good experiences. Discussions on the forums sometimes relay horror stories of freeloaders refusing to leave, or leeching excessively on the resources of the host. There was one instance where a guest told me that "couchsurfing is all about the free stuff", and suggested a system to be put up where guests can rate hosts in terms of friendliness, cleanliness and other indicators of a good host. (As a host offering free hospitality, I was taken aback and slightly offended, but I realised that for research purposes this was good data). There are traces of racism in interactions with other couchsurfers, and more so on forum discussions; also, it is not unusual to hear of sexual encounters between hosts and guests.

How the couchsurfers behave in reality is not really the focal point of this chapter. Instead, the point is that, as a member of the community, one has to present oneself as someone who understands the rules, to help in telling the story of a trustworthy couchsurfer. A further point to consider is that a couchsurfer who is attractive to other couchsurfers is not only someone who plays within the rules of the community; it is also important that he/she is able to contribute to the cultural exchange in a meaningful way, through interesting life experiences, skills and knowledges that are able to be shared. I propose that the package of a desirable couchsurfer is evaluated through his/her accumulated subcultural capital. The examination of taboos on Couchsurfing.org also suggests that mere cosmopolitanism is not sufficient – one has to have the qualities of a reflexive cosmopolite who upholds certain emotional and ethical commitments on interactions with people of other cultures.

In other words, couchsurfers manage their impressions (à la Goffman, 1959, who views social interactions as performances on stage, where people are actors and audiences at the same time, both managing and forming impressions) based on reflexive cosmopolitanism, giving and giving off expressions of being an open-minded, travel-savvy individual to be socially accepted and trusted. The operative word, "performing", can give off the connotation that there is deception involved, however I would like to clarify that this is not implied: as argued by Edgley (2003), there is a difference between the dramaturgical principle and dramaturgical awareness. The dramaturgical principle is that when people engage in social interaction, they engage in presentation of self, universally and in all situations. However, they may not be dramaturgically aware, i.e. the actor may not be aware of the performance that is going on; the level of awareness may be dependent on factors such as the significance of the audience.

If reflexive cosmopolitanism is performed, what is the stage? As couchsurfers interact online and offline, they can present themselves on both communication channels. As mentioned earlier, there are two types of subcultural capital, as explained by Thornton (1996), i.e. embodied and objectified. For couchsurfers, it can be observed that embodied subcultural capital includes the ability to exhibit cultural competence in the form of politeness and respectfulness, interest in learning and sharing cultural differences and commonalities, and an awareness of the taboos mentioned earlier. This is manifested online through the efficacy of writing requests and profiles, and offline in face-to-face interactions such as conversations and general-impression management. The couchsurfer learns about do's and don'ts through tips provided by Couchsurfing.org,[2] by asking for advice in the forum groups (there are some groups that cater specifically to this, e.g. "Advice for Hosts", "Reference Writing Support", etc.), or simply through trial and error. In the case of objectified subcultural capital, there are rich possibilities for presenting oneself as a world traveller and a

2 | See http://www.couchsurfing.org/tips.html

competent cosmopolite. One is able to specify countries visited, languages spoken, "one amazing thing I've seen or done", couchsurfing experiences, pictures (which often depict the couchsurfer in exotic places or surrounded by multicultural friends), etc. References, friend links, vouches and various community designations (such as couchsurfing ambassadorships) are also acquired with experience, and are displayed prominently in one's profile, suggesting one's cosmopolitan stance.

Most respondents interviewed had experience in hosting or surfing, and had clear ideas on the qualities of a "good" couchsurfer, and how to go about presenting oneself as one. However, I have been approached by first-timers who are interested in trying out the system, who ask me questions on "the best way to write a request", how to read a profile, what information to put on the profile, what to expect from the experience, what the etiquette is in terms of showing appreciation to the hosts or entertaining a guest, etc. This provides an interesting insight into how new couchsurfers learn to recognise what behaviours and attitudes are normal within the community, and also how to form and manage impressions when one immerses oneself in the system. Having subcultural capital means that one has to know the appropriate cultural signals to emit, and also recognise the signals when received. In the context of couchsurfing, ample tools and space are provided, online and offline, for these cosmopolites to exercise these skills, and to mingle with other cosmopolites within the community of travellers.

Creating the context for trust

So how does accumulating subcultural capital via performing reflexive cosmopolitanism link back to the issue of trust? I propose that a community of reflexive cosmopolites (imagined or real) helps to create a metanarrative of trust based on meaningful interactions that rise above petty narrow-mindedness or opportunism; the metanarrative in turn influences the actors' behaviours when they manage and form impressions based on general principles of reflexive cosmopolitanism, causing the overall impression of the community to be perceived as trustworthy.

As I mentioned above, one of the ways for actors to make "the leap of faith" is through creating narratives in the trustor's mind, enabling him/her to trust as if the outcomes were favourable. This is a salient piece of the puzzle that explains how favourable conditions for building trust are created. As argued by Möllering, "trust does not rest on objective reality but on 'illusion'. It rests on the fiction of a reality in which social uncertainty and vulnerability are unproblematic". The trustor and trustee work together to create this fiction in the trustor's head, through the trustee presenting him/herself as being trustworthy, and the trustor forming the impression with available information. I'd like to suggest the idea that judgements based on user-to-user communication are bolstered with a metanarrative, "a global or totalizing cultural narrative schema which orders and explains knowledge and experience" (Stephens, 1998) of the ideal image of a cosmopolitan community that is authentic and reflexive.

The metanarrative of couchsurfing as a community of reflexive cosmopolites helps to tell the story of individual couchsurfers who are likely to be (or aspire to be) widely travelled, and who know the rules of engagement within the couchsurfing community and beyond. A romantic view can be constructed, of couchsurfers having "the spirit of people who hitchhike the world" (said in an admiring manner by 26-year-old Tony, a Taiwanese-American respondent), and who have "a distinct ethical orientation towards selflessness, worldliness and communitarianism [...] driving much of the contemporary environmental, anti-war and anti-globalization movements" (Kendall et al., 2009:22-23). It is entirely conceivable that one who upholds these ideals and sentiments would be someone who would not pose a risk of inflicting bodily harm, or who would be an unpleasant guest or host. The metanarrative builds a strong foundation for other narratives (that enable trust) to be formed, and one who decides to use the couchsurfing website would already have reduced the gap needed to make the leap of faith to trust individual members.

The metanarrative establishes social norms within the community, influencing the behaviour of members through socialisation. The social norms and the metanarrative are in a mutually reinforcing cycle. The metanarrative makes it clear that certain behaviours are "in the spirit of couchsurfing", and certain behaviours are not. Having a normative framework as a moral compass (for behaviours deemed right and wrong within the system) reduces uncertainty in the interactions between members of the community. One knows what is appropriate and what is not, and makes the assumption that other members of the community understand that as well, as demonstrated in the section on the social taboos of couchsurfing. The possibility of sanctioning misbehaving members (through leaving negative references) also sustains confidence in the community in general. These measures make it easier for narratives of trustworthiness (or untrustworthiness, for that matter) to be formed.

Established social norms can also influence the behaviours of members within the society. A good example of how performing cosmopolitanism is able to affect behaviour is to look at the act of leaving negative references. According to Adamic et al. (2011), there is a "near absence" of negative references, and the ratio of positive to negative references on Couchsurfing.org is 2500:1. Common reasons for not putting a negative reference include: fear of a retaliatory negative reference, reluctance to smear someone else's reputation, unwillingness to give a negative rating contrary to a long list of positive remarks, etc. If interpreted according to this theoretical framework, negative references tend to deplete one's subcultural capital (as a black mark on one's profile), which is why retaliatory negative references are such a threat. Also, the very act of complaining about the experience implies that one is not open-minded enough to enjoy cultural exchange.

This might explain why couchsurfers have a high threshold of tolerance for uncomfortable experiences, with respondents reflecting that the experience should be "really, really bad" (Sonja, a Dutch respondent in her twenties) to warrant a negative reference. When asked about these situations, it is usually something that is beyond individual or cultural differences (for instance, in terms of personal hygiene, differing political views, etc.) and is overtly deviant in general, such as extreme racism, theft, rape, etc. These fall under the clear category of wrong behaviours that transcend cultural oddities.

Although there are other factors that deter the writing of negative references, such as fear of confrontation or the unwillingness to be ungrateful for someone's hospitality, I would argue that the societal pressure to be a reflexive cosmopolite (maintaining a "clean" profile, and to be seen as one who celebrates cultural differences instead of complaining about them) provides a big demotivation for leaving negative references. The absence of negative references then reinforces the image of a trustworthy website and community. Through intangible and tangible ways, performing cosmopolitanism as subcultural capital helps build a context that encourages trust. The metanarrative of couchsurfers as being reflexive, cosmopolitan individuals paints a trustworthy and ethical collective image; couchsurfers, having to live up to that collective image, strategize their behaviours and attitudes within the context of the system.

Although it is tempting to make a blanket statement that the metanarrative dictates the narratives of trustworthiness, and provides a definite guide to whether or not one trusts (based on the trustee's ownership of subcultural capital), the case is not so simple. It is apparent that although people who surf couches with the sole motivation of budget travel are scorned in many segments of the couchsurfing community, there are critics who see such judgemental views as hypocrisy. In a widely circulated blog post on critiques of couchsurfing,[3] the anonymous author wrote that free accommodation is the primary goal of couchsurfing, and that cultural exchange is a positive, but not necessary, consequence. He/she argued that hosts and surfers (especially surfers) are compelled to spend time together in the name of cultural exchange, even when they do not enjoy it:

> One of the most disconcerting things about couchsurfing is the pressure to hang out with people when you would not otherwise want to do so. Not in a positive way as in talking to people you would not normally talk to and gaining new insight, but rather a pressure for people who simply don't get along to pretend they like and are interested in learning more about each other. Every user is encouraged to fill in their profile with as much detail as possible not unlike a MySpace page. The majority of these details have absolutely no relevance to requesting to stay on someone's couch for a few days either from a hosting or surfing perspective. This is actually enforced in some ways with quite a few people stating that they will not even consider hosting you unless your profile is substantially filled out. Didn't list your favorite movies and books? Then forget it. It is this need and want to know everything about people that strikes me as being so very hypocritical and fake. If you want to get to know someone then talk to them when they arrive; don't use their lists of favorite movies and books or philosophies and political opinions as the only indicator.

This quote reinforces the idea of the metanarrative that exists in the couchsurfing community, which directly affects how people behave and fill in their profiles. According to this writer, it appears that the metanarrative that exists on Couchsurfing.org does not apply to other similar hospitality exchange websites. He or she continued:

---

3 | http://allthatiswrong.wordpress.com/2010/01/24/a-criticism-of-couchsurfing-and-review-of-alternatives/#free

> The level of emphasis that these different [hospex] sites place on free accommodation is perhaps where they differ most. For couchsurfing while free accommodation exists as a point, it is not at all defined by it and it may well be a minor point. There are a great many people on couchsurfing who are using the service to save money even if they don't say so. For GlobalFreeloaders the emphasis is without a doubt on free accommodation. This is evident in the lack of profiles and general philosophy of the people on the site. Instead of checking out individual profiles, you mass mail the people in any city you think may like to host you, and anyone interested gets back to you. Personally, I find this to be a whole lot more honest and refreshing than the somewhat forced "let's be friends!" philosophy pushed by Couchsurfing. For Hospitality Club the emphasis seems about equal to that of seeing new cultures. I have not had a chance to use BeWelcome or Tripping however at a glance they seem to have a similar philosophie [sic] to Hospitality Club.

The data reflect the existence of a dominant discourse (and, therefore, counter-discourses) of reflexive cosmopolitanism as normative behaviour within the system. This is due to two fundamentally different ways of viewing Couchsurfing.org – as a community, or as a service. It is noted in Heesakkers's work (2008) that some users had reservations over the rapid growth of Couchsurfing.org, indicating that there might be a danger that quantity would surpass quality. What used to be a "community" would become more of a "service". The distinction is important because the sense of responsibility and ownership would affect how the website is used; e.g. a person who perceived himself/herself to be part of the community would be more inclined to protect its safety and common ideologies. The concern of these users has been confirmed by another study through an inherent value-testing of Couchsurfing.org (Lauterbach et al., 2008), comparing the experiences of new and experienced users of the website. One of the major findings was that existing and loyal users prized friendship and community, whereas new users viewed the site as more of a service.

The resulting interaction can be very disconcerting, between one who holds on to the set of beliefs and values reflected by the metanarrative and another who doesn't. I have since realised that actors look for a good match between two people with similar expectations of couchsurfing. Seasoned couchsurfers consciously look for people who match them in this sense, to avoid unpleasant encounters. Secondly, the metanarrative, as it is propagated and reinforced by the community, tends to affect one's trust-building more when the trustor views Couchsurfing.org as a community. Conversely, when one sees Couchsurfing.org as a service, the metanarrative does not matter as much to the individual. As the member base of couchsurfing grows at an exponential rate, it will be a challenge for the organisation to propagate the metanarrative to its members, and facilitate a better match between members who would hold different levels of expectations.

Conclusion

In this chapter I have studied the online community Couchsurfing.org to explore how macro-level contexts encourage trust-building in an online community environment. Actors learn and perform reflexive cosmopolitanism (a form of cosmopolitanism that presumably celebrates diversity and intercultural interaction in a "genuine" way), emitting and receiving socially desirable signals as a form of subcultural capital. Through defining and accumulating subcultural capital within the community, a metanarrative of couchsurfers being genuine cosmopolites is formed, creating a good foundation to build other narratives at a micro-level and create an image of trustworthiness for the trustor. At the same time, in the process of accumulating subcultural capital, actors are socially pressured to be tolerant of cultural or individual differences, affecting the motivation to leave negative feedback online, which further reinforces the image of the trustworthiness of the community. It is also found that counter-narratives to the metanarrative exist, and the level of importance of the metanarrative depends on whether one views Couchsurfing.org as a community or a service. To facilitate effective trust-building, the platform should propagate the metanarrative to its expanding member base, and optimise matches between members with different expectations and interpretations of the website.

In a social network site where connections form online and are extended offline, purposive accumulation of subcultural capital by the individual actor (through building a strong profile and communicating online and offline in a socially accepted way) builds trust, which is then converted into social capital. The macro-level context of trust is important, but tells only half the story, as it does not address trust at the individual level, where couchsurfers make actual trusting decisions. This paper is part of a larger research project (my doctoral dissertation), and only discusses the macro-level context due to the limited space available. Micro-level interactions and trust-building processes are under examination, and will be addressed in future work.

References

Adamic, L.A., Lauterbach, D., Teng, C.-Y. and Ackerman, M.S. (2011) *Rating friends without making enemies.* Paper presented at the 5th International AAAI Conference on Weblogs and Social Media, Barcelona, Spain.

Beazley, H. (2003) "The construction and protection of individual and collective identities by street children and youth in Indonesia". *Children, Youth and Environments* 13(1). Retrieved from http://colorado.edu/journals/cye.

Beck, U. (2003) "Rooted cosmopolitanism: emerging from a rivalry of distinctions". In U. Beck, N. Sznaider and R. Winter (eds.) *Global America?: The cultural consequences of globalization.* Liverpool: Liverpool University Press.

Bialski, P. (2007) *Intimate tourism: friendships in a state of mobility – the case of the online hospitality network.* Warsaw: University of Warsaw.

Bialski, P. and Batorski, D. (2010) "From online familiarity to offline trust: how a virtual community creates familiarity and trust between strangers". In P. Zaphiris and C.S. Ang (eds.) *Social computing and virtual communities.* Boca Raton: Taylor & Francis.

Bullen, E. and Kenway, J. (2005) "Bourdieu, subcultural capital and risky girlhood". *Theory and Research in Education* 3(1):47-61.

Coleman, J.S. (1990) *Foundations of social theory.* Cambridge, MA: Harvard University Press.

Edgley, C. (2003) "The dramaturgical genre". In L.T. Reynolds and N.J. Reynolds (eds.) *The handbook of symbolic interactionism.* Boulder, CO: AltaMira Press.

Gelder, K. (2005). "Introduction: The field of subcultural studies". In K. Gelder (ed.), *The Subcultures Reader.* New York: Routledge.

Germann Molz, J. (2007) "Cosmopolitans on the couch: mobile hospitality and the Internet". In S.G.J. Germann Molz (ed.) *Mobilizing hospitality: the ethics of social relations in a mobile world.* Hampshire: Ashgate, pp.65-80.

Giulianotti, R. (2002) "Supporters, followers, fans, and flaneurs: a taxonomy of spectator identities in football". *Journal of Sport and Social Issues* 26(1):25-46.

Goffman, E. (1959) *The presentation of Self in everyday life*. Harmondsworth: Penguin.

Kendall, G., Woodward, I. and Skrbis, Z. (2009) *The sociology of cosmopolitanism: globalization, identity, culture and government*. New York: Palgrave Macmillan.

Lamont, M. and Lareau, A. (1988) "Cultural capital: allusions, gaps and glissandos in recent theoretical developments". *Sociological Theory* 6(2):153-168.

Lareau, A. and Weininger, E.B. (2003) "Cultural capital in educational research: a critical assessment". *Theory and Society* 32(5):567-606.

Möllering, G. (2006) *Trust: reason, routine reflexivity*. Oxford: Elsevier, Ltd.

Ostberg, J. (2007) "The linking value of subcultural capital: constructing the Stockholm Brat enclave". In R.V.K.B. Cova and A. Shankar (eds.) *Consumer tribes*. Oxford: Butterworth-Heinemann.

Robson, K. (2009) "Teenage time use as investment in cultural capital". In K. Robson and C. Sanders (eds.) *Quantifying theory: Pierre Bourdieu*. New York: Springer Science & Business Media.

Rosen, D., Lafontaine, P.R. and Hendrickson, B. (2011) "Couchsurfing: belonging and trust in a globally cooperative online social network". *New Media & Society* 13(6): 981-998.

Stephens, J. and McCallum, R. (1998) *Retelling stories, framing culture: traditional story and metanarratives in children's literature*. New York: Garland.

Tan, J.-E. (2010) "The leap of faith from online to offline: an exploratory study of Couchsurfing.org". In A. Acquisti, S. Smith and A.-R. Sadeghi (eds.) *Trust and trustworthy computing*. Berlin: Springer, pp.367-380.

Thornton, S. (1996) *Club cultures: music, media and subcultural capital*. Hanover: New England University Press.

Tran, L.D. (2009) *Trust in an online hospitality network: an interpretive study of the couchsurfing project*. Oslo University College, Parma University and Tallinn University.

Tulloch, J. and Lupton, D. (2003) *Risk and everyday life*. London: Sage.

8. Online to Offline Social Networking: Contextualising Sociality Today Through Couchsurfing.org

Paula Bialski

Introduction[1]

Based on a five-year ethnographic study of couchsurfers, and insights from over 3500 open-ended survey responses, this chapter introduces one of the first "online to offline" social networking technologies in order to define the importance of such technologies in the life-course of Internet users. "Online to offline" technologies, where people meet online in order to interact offline, are affecting the processes of sociality today – the way people trust and distrust strangers, the way they accept others and reject the rest, and the ways in which interactions are formed and developed. People who use couchsurfing create ways of engaging in interaction with strangers – and these methods of trusting and interacting with an unknown Other are repeated as people continually engage in other forms of online to offline technologies.

The year I joined Couchsurfing.org (hereafter "Couchsurfing"), the website was just four months old. It was early in 2005, and I opened the doors of my small flat in Warsaw, Poland to a slew of strangers. At the time, the website had fewer than 30,000 registered members worldwide. A year later, the founder of the website, Casey Fenton, came to visit Warsaw (April 2006) and, along with two other website programmers, stayed on my

1 | Parts of this chapter were derived from my doctoral thesis, entitled *Becoming Intimately Mobile* (2012) that investigates couchsurfing and online hitchhiking websites in order to understand the affects of mobility on intimacy, trust and strangerhood.

couch and living-room floor. During that time, I was a master's student of sociology, and started to discuss the ways in which the website was used as a tool to meet offline and offered the user a way to engage in diverse forms of sociality and hospitality that went beyond the merely dating and romantic match-making websites that had also emerged during the early 2000s.

In the summer of 2006, Casey invited me to spend two months living with a group of volunteers at the "Couchsurfing Collective" in Montreal – a temporary commune of sorts established in order to remodel, debug and improve the website. Based on a co-working environment model exported from their early days in the Silicon Valley dot-com boom, the "Collective's" members worked out of the first floor of a row house in Montreal's mile-end district, with computers and programmers packed into a single room, intensively typing away on their keyboards. By June 2006, the news had spread throughout the 40,000-strong couchsurfing global community that a Collective had been established to help improve the website; throughout the summer, volunteers and eager couchsurfers would come through the house for a day, or a few weeks at a time, lending help in the form of baking or programming skills. While in Montreal, I created an online survey which was conducted between my stay at the Collective and continued until March 2007. This online survey was programmed into the website, and was made available to users through their individual profiles by adding an extra tab named "My Survey" to their profile. I couldn't have found a more ideal place to do my research. In those months, a little over 3600 couchsurfers responded to my survey – answering 24 questions about their motivations to travel using couchsurfing, the duration of their host-guest interactions, why they (don't) stay in touch with their hosts and/or guests, and other questions relating to the nature of their interaction on the website.

This was a fertile period for me as a researcher – gaining insight into the motivations that drove couchsurfers to become part of the community, and the experiences and practices that shaped their views of that community. The research I gathered at the Collective, which included 20 in-depth interviews, a number of notes and informal discussions and observations and the massive amounts of data from my online survey response, all helped me complete my master's and doctoral dissertations. That being said, this short chapter is meant merely to present insights from my years of research in order to gain an overall introduction into online-to-offline technologies. Specifically, my observations and open-ended online survey responses help illustrate the reasons why people engage in online-to-offline social networking technologies in the first place.

Theorising online to offline

Globally, over two-billion people[2] use the Internet daily, and in the United States an average user is online for six hours a day. Those who log online and stay online engage in a variety of activities with other people that keep them in a virtual world – chatting, shopping, reading blogs, selling products, playing games and social networking with their offline friends, to name a few. Some of these two-billion users use the Internet as a tool to engage in sociality offline. While the Internet is associated with time spent online, seldom is the attention of users or social researchers turned to the way in which the Internet is sometimes merely a tool, a medium, to create contact between others offline.

Not only have people been using computers more and more to coordinate meetings offline, people have also been couchsurfing more. Since I started studying Couchsurfing in 2007, the website has grown in size, from around 50,000 users to close to five-million.[3] Moreover, the social networking site Facebook has come to play an increasingly important part in many people's social lives, in particular by enabling "informal" forms of couchsurfing and ride-sharing via recommendation systems using friends-of-friends and other weak ties.

Through these websites, an increasing number of strangers are meeting, and subsequently experiencing hospitality and closeness. Based on internal statistics, Couchsurfing claims that weekly it helps create around 40,024 real-life "introductions" between users of the site (31,185 of these are "positive" versus only 84 "negative"). Every week, 1,189,634 couches are advertised as "available", and 189,879 people state that they have made a "close friendship" connection through couchsurfing.

While hospitality networks like Couchsurfing were among the first websites designed for online-to-offline social networking, a large variety of such networks, in all shapes and sizes, exist today. Online-to-offline so-

2 | Internet Usage and World Population Statistics are for 31 March 2011. http://www.Internetworldstats.com/stats.htm

3 | Couchsurfing statistics, www.couchsurfing.org

cial-networking technologies include websites or smartphone applications which allow users to connect to unknown others through an Internet connection with the intention of meeting offline. These online-to-offline technologies can be online hospitality networks like Couchsurfing, or house-swapping websites where people login to exchange homes for a temporary period with other people in remote places. One of the most popular, and perhaps the first, online-to-offline technologies are dating websites where people meet online in order to date or start a romantic relationship offline. Other examples are transport-oriented online-to-offline technologies like online hitchhiking and carpooling websites (ex. Mitfahrgelegenheit.de or carpooling.pl), where drivers search for passengers to help alleviate transportation costs between cities. Online-to-offline technologies also include classified advertisement websites like gumtree.co.uk or craigslist.com – where often anonymous users advertise various things like new and second-hand goods, accommodation, services, jobs, classes and sex. Hobby-based meet-up websites, such as meetup.com, and various gaming websites where people meet online in order to meet offline with the purpose of engaging in or discussing a common hobby can also be defined as online-to-offline technologies.

The number of new technologies that are creating close interactions and enabling the coordination of people offline is growing at a fast pace. Smartphones are linking up with online social networking services like Facebook's "Places" or Four Square (www.facebook.com/places; www.foursquare.com), and engage people, their mobile devices and the Internet in social networks which are constantly updating "hot spots" in a certain city: places to meet, places to eat, places to dance, places to avoid dancing.

The importance of online-to-offline technologies like Four Square, Facebook Places and Couchsurfing (which will be discussed in this chapter) is the way in which they affect the processes of sociality – the ways people trust and distrust strangers, the ways they accept others and reject the rest, and the ways in which interactions are formed and developed. People who use Couchsurfing create ways of interacting with strangers – and these methods of trusting and interacting with an unknown Other are repeated as people continually engage in other forms of online-to-offline technologies.

The ways in which people make choices, or decide who to interact with offline and who to trust offline, were among the major concerns in Internet research during the 1980s and 1990s. Research focusing on the effects of telephones versus computer-mediated communication (CMC) in the persistence or dissipation of pre-interaction expectancies (Walther et al., 2010) suggests that CMC was at times superior in transmitting positive impressions to other interactants (Walther, 1995).

Not only were online interaction, romance, flirting, friendship and acquaintanceship becoming topics of interest, certain research was also looking into the impact of Internet-initiated relationships. For example, Parks and Roberts, in their survey of relationships created via real-time, text-based virtual environments known as MOOs (Multi-User Dimensions, Object Oriented), showed that a third of all relationships resulted in face-to face meetings (Parks and Roberts, 1998). Other early Internet research found similar insights, stating that "relationships that started online rarely stayed there" (Parks and Floyd, 1996:92), and where "about a third had used the telephone, the postal service, or face-to-face communication to contact their on-line friends" (ibid.). Early on, those researching CMC friendships termed online relationships which continued offline as "migratory".

Researchers studying the Internet from a computer science or communications orientation were "guided by the engineering concept of 'communication bandwidth'" and "assumed at a meta-theoretical level that the reduction in social cues during Internet communication compared to the presumably richer face-to-face situation (with all of its attendant nonverbal, expressive cues) must necessarily have negative effects on social interaction" (Bargh, 2002:2). The "reduced cues" or "diminished bandwidth" of Internet communication, when compared to face-to-face settings, created, as Bargh terms it, "an atmosphere of ambiguity" (Bargh, 2002: 3).

Only ten years later, as CMC became socially adopted at home and for work and leisure, did strictly face-to-face communication cease to be the only method of communication with another person. Due to the prominence of CMC technology in people's lives, Turkle has recently explained that humans have developed new skills of interaction. Turkle suggests that the values of human sociality shift as "technology offers us substitutes for connecting with each other face-to-face" (Turkle, 2001:11). She writes, "We don't ask the open ended 'How are you?' Instead, we ask the more limited 'where are you?' and 'what's up?' These are good questions for getting someone's location and making a simple plan. They are not so good for opening a dialogue about complexity of feeling. We are increasingly connected to each other but oddly more alone: in intimacy, new solitudes" (ibid.:19).

At the beginning of research into the Internet, Internet pessimists and journalists also warned that isolation, not connectivity, would be the result of CMC: "While all this razzle-dazzle connects us electronically, it disconnects us from each other, having us 'interfacing' more with computers and TV screens than looking in the face of our fellow human beings" (Hightower, 1994).[4]

Noll (1995:191) also warned that "the information superhighway has not been as super as many have promised. The many potholes and washed out bridges have jolted our sense of reality". In the mid-1990s, Kraut et al. (1998) reported negative effects of using the Internet on social involvement and psychological well-being among new Internet users. This was a big issue among researchers at the time – linking Internet use to social and psychological problems like addiction (Kandell, 1998) and depression (Young and Roberts, 1998).

Other research suggest almost opposite conclusions, claiming that CMC does help to enrich lives, and brings people closer together. There is "less evidence that the Internet is pushing people away from traditional social ties or making them less trusting" (Uslaner, 2000:22). In a follow-up study, Kraut et al. found that negative effects of Internet use dispersed, showing that the Internet can lead to positive effects on communication, social involvement and well-being (Kraut et al., 2002). According to several large-scale American and international surveys of Internet users, the great majority of respondents consider Internet use to have improved their lives (McKenna and Bargh, 2000), that a substantial proportion (over 50 %) of over 600 Internet users surveyed had brought an Internet relationship into their real life (i.e. met in person), and that over 20 % of those respondents had formed a romantic relationship and were now living with or engaged to someone they met on the Internet (McKenna, 1998).

Thus, the Internet proved even to be helpful in offline relationships. Bargh et al. found that in first-time encounters an individual will be liked more if the encounter takes place in an Internet chat room than if the two strangers were to meet face to face. In their study, those who first met on the Internet and then talked face to face liked one another more than did those who met face to face in both encounters" (Bargh et al., 2002:65).

4 | See: http://www.jimhightower.com/node/2134

WHO GOES ONLINE-TO-OFFLINE AND WHY?

One founder of the Couchsurfing website explained that couchsurfing "is not just a free couch. This promises intense, frequent, diverse interactions" (interview response, 2006). It is the urgency, passion and sense of intensity in these types of "crossroad meetings" that the online-to-offline relationship often provides.

A Finnish interview respondent commented on the reasons for such intensity, stating:

> Of course the process has to be quicker because they're only staying for a while so it's more intense, deeper than it would be when meeting random strangers on the street. [...] But with Couchsurfers it would be more intense [...] it's just because you only know that they're going to be gone soon. When I talk to people I do not wish to discuss the superficial things like 'what went on in the football game' or 'which model has the biggest boobs', so with Couchsurfer there's an excuse to avoid all that stuff because they're only there for a short time. So you get closer faster.

The fact that the guest will be "gone soon" or their stay "fleeting and transient" also seems to instigate an urgency to speed up the familiarisation process or degree of social penetration, still creating "social relations of ephemeral but intense encounters" (Wittel, 2001:72).

The online-to-offline also feeds the compulsion to be proximate, because, as some argue, only face-to-face interaction provides a sensory richness of interaction (Boden and Molotch, 1994). A 19-year-old Polish survey respondent explained that, "there's nothing better than getting to know about new culture and people by face to face contact".

Numerous survey respondents explained that meeting face-to-face created in depth, all-sensory contact with another person. "Buddies, as every chat addict knows, come and go, switch in and out – but there are always a few of them on the line itching to drown silence in 'messages'. [...] We belong to talking, not to what is talked about" (Bauman, 2003:34). This chatter is what the intimately mobile wish to avoid through tangible, all-sensory, face-to-face emotional encounters that provide "depth" and "authenticity".

Another 27-year-old survey respondent explained that he was motivated to use Couchsurfing because it provided him with "different perspectives in life, a friend, a familiar face to see when you are out of your home visiting other city, someone with your own interests and someone with totally different interests…" Couchsurfers are often drawn to the idea either out of an understanding of the practice (i.e. they have created informal networks of hospitality, where they used to stay on the couches of friends-of-friends or hosted people they met in a pub or at a party), or a desire to engage in a practice that promises friendship and trust – an alternative to the risk society under individualistic, consumer capitalism: a utopian altruism. Moreover, while one could possibly come to the conclusion that people want to become part of Couchsurfing because they have the time, financial resources and accommodation to host another individual, this is often not the case. Couchsurfers have many faces. They can be families, single bachelors living in bachelor apartments, young mothers, students living in residence, farmers. Calling "couchsurfing" by its name is deceiving – visitors sleep in tents, on the floor, on blow-up mattresses, on children's beds (the children then sleep with their parents), in a barn – or sometimes share a bed with the host. Thus, a person's lifestyle is irrelevant – if somebody is interested in the idea of couchsurfing, they will arrange their lives around their practice. When the website was first created, and for the duration this research was conducted, the website's slogan was a call to "Participate in Creating a Better World – One Couch at a Time" (the website's slogan changed to "CouchSurfing helps you meet and adventure with new friends around the world" in 2011). Thus, in order for users to be able to feel safe using this type of online-to-offline technology, they must identify themselves with the ideology behind the website. The barebones structure of this type of exchange promises new users a cheap way to travel – a free couch. Yet, Couchsurfing aims to weed out this type of utilitarianism while providing an ideology with a free couch – "this is not just a free couch. This promises intense, frequent, diverse interactions", stated the founder of the website in an interview with me in Montreal.

Ideology in Practice

Couchsurfing is based on a common purpose and ideology, where members express the belief that opening up one's home to strangers will provide them with various cultural, educational and self-reflective benefits. What is also worth noting is that trustfulness becomes a mandatory practice in order to become part of this community. In other words, you cannot be a couchsurfer if you don't want to trust another person enough to let them into your own home, your own private space.

Those who gain the desire to join the website first have to understand what a virtual community is and how it functions and, quite basically, must be able to log onto a website. Those who desire to join Couchsurfing must understand and trust the system that is the Internet. Without already holding a narrative of the Internet, belief in the functionality of this type of virtual community is impossible.

The process of self-presentation online is an important aspect in relational development offline. Couchsurfers must establish an online profile of themselves, and this profile communicates information about them which is crucial in creating a sense of knowledge about the other person, which in turn influences familiarity. The profile also plays a crucial role in a user's social navigation through the website, when he/she chooses whom to initiate contact with. As the average age of Couchsurfer members is 27, and 70 % of users are from Europe or North America, most new couchsurfers have a high level of media literacy and are proficient in navigating websites.

Couchsurfing also does not guarantee relationship longevity. Because couchsurfers are highly mobile, living on a here-today-gone-tomorrow basis, keeping in touch with their previous hosts or guests means interacting with them online – precisely what they do not want to be doing. The very reasons for engaging in online-to-offline technologies – the desire for face-to-face proximity, the feeling of home-when-away, closeness, intensity, cultural exchange – can bring people closer together, but also prevent them from keeping in touch. People who are more interested in using online-to-offline technologies to meet offline will not go online. When asked why she does not keep in touch with her previous hosts or guests, a 30-year-old Finnish survey respondent explained that she "strongly prefer(s) face-to-face discussions to exchanging emails or chatting online". Another, 28-year-old Brazilian survey respondent explained: "I don't like emails very much, but would love to have a face-to-face friendship with most of them".

One 31-year-old American survey respondent said:

> With the power of the Internet and today's communication systems making the world 'smaller' we seem to sometimes lose the value of interpersonal relationships. It's easier to shoot off an email, rather than write a personal note, have a chat over IM instead of a phone call [...] opening your home to someone is so very

personal (at least to me), and through that I hope to nurture a greater respect and knowledge of this global community in which we reside.

Going offline, in her case, also promised that she would not lose sight of the importance of interpersonal relationships: the all-sensory cues, the trust, the emotions and the adventure that meeting people offline provides.

Conclusion

This chapter is intended to be an introduction into the sociality formed within the hospitality community site Couchsurfing.org, discussing the motivations that users have in using a tool to meet people offline. The intensity of interaction, the all-sensory richness of face-to-face communication and the promise of meeting and trusting people in a "global community" have all been discussed. Couchsurfing thus cannot be looked at as just another social-networking website, but rather must be defined as an online-to-offline social-networking technology. Such technologies are a significant part of the Internet landscape, and must be taken into account when studying the needs of Internet users, the impact the Internet has on social capital, trust, processes of interaction, face-to-face proximity, online identity-building and various other phenomena of interaction.

References

Bargh, J.A. (2002) "Beyond simple truths: the human-Internet interaction". *Journal of Social Issues* 58:1-8.

Bargh, J.A. and McKenna, K.Y.A. (2004) "The Internet and social life". *Annual Review of Psychology* 55:573-590.

Bargh, J.A., McKenna, K.Y.A. and Fitzsimmons, G.M. (2002) "Can you see the real me? Relationship formation and development on the Internet". *Journal of Social Issues* 58:33-48.

Bauman, Z. (2003) *Liquid love: on the frailty of human bonds.* Cambridge: Polity Press.

Boden, D. and Molotch, H.L. (1994) "The compulsion of proximity". In R. Friedland and D. Boden (eds.) *Space, time and modernity.* London: University of California Press.

Hightower, J. (1994) "Roadkill on the information superhighway". http://www.jimhightower.com/node/2134 (accessed 21 November 2012).

Kandell, J.J. (1998) "Internet addiction on campus: the vulnerability of college students". *CyberPsychology & Behavior* 1:11-17.

Kraut, R.E., Patterson, M., Lundmark, V., Kiesler, S., Mukopadhyay, T. and Scherlis, W. (1998) "Internet paradox: a social technology that reduces social involvement and psychological well-being?" *American Psychologist* 53:1017-1031.

McKenna, K.Y.A. and Bargh, J.A. (2000) "Plan 9 from cyberspace: the implications of the Internet for personality and social psychology". *February* 4: 57-75.

McKenna, K.Y.A. (1998) "The computers that bind: relationship formation on the Internet". Unpublished doctoral dissertation, Ohio University.

Noll, M. (1995) *Highway of dreams: a critical view along the information superhighway*. Hillsdale, NJ: Lawrence Erlbaum Associates, Inc.

Orgad, S. (2006) "From online to offline and back: moving from online to offline relationships with research informants". In C. Hine (ed.) *Virtual methods: issues in social research on the Internet*. New York: Berg.

Parks, M.R. and Floyd, K. (1996) "Making friends in cyberspace". *Journal of Communication* 46:80-97.

Parks, M.R. and Roberts, L.D. (1998) "'Making MOOsic': the development of personal relationships on-line and a comparison to their off-line counterparts". *Journal of Social & Personal Relationships* 15:517-530.

Turkle, S. (2011) *Alone together: why we expect more from technology and less from each other*. New York: Basic Books.

Uslaner, E.M. (2000) "Social capital and the Net". *Communications of the ACM* 43:60-64.

Uslaner, E.M. (2000) "Trust, civic engagement, and the Internet". Paper presented at Joint Sessions of the European Consortium for Political Research, Workshop on Electronic Democracy: Mobilisation, Organisation, and Participation via New ICTs, University of Grenoble.

Walther, J.B. (1995) "Relational aspects of computer-mediated communication: experimental observations over time". *Organization Science* 6:186-203.

Wittel, A. (2001) "Towards a networked sociality". *Theory Culture and Society* 18:51-76.

Young, K.S. and Rogers, R.C. (1998) "The relationship between depression and Internet addiction". *CyberPsychology & Behavior* 1:25-28.

9. Anthropology and Couchsurfing – Variations on a Theme (An Afterword)

Nelson Graburn

In reading the exciting and original chapters of this book, one soon gets the impression that couchsurfing involves many of the central themes of anthropology – reciprocity and the morality of the gift, social boundaries, friendship and kinship, modernity and contact zones. Couchsurfing is a nostalgic attempt using the internet to resurrect the kind of pre-capitalist travel and hospitality found among many of the peoples whom anthropologists study. Our understanding of couchsurfing is enhanced by its commonalities with the practice of anthropology – extended travels, cultural learning through participant observation, power differentials and trust (Powdermaker, 1966), misunderstandings, and implicit rites of passage. Indeed, the guest-surfer is in the ideal situation to do inside research (see p. 9-10) on a variant of their "own culture" (cf. Okely, 1996).

Reciprocity and relationships

Hospitality is one form of alliance which includes marriage, peace-making, commensality, gift exchange and even forms of speech, involving rules which allow relationships and communities to persist over time. The word *host* is a close cognate to *guest*,[1] and couchsurfing ideally equates the two, alternating with each other. In many traditional societies, hospitality towards a stranger was required; a modern interpretation is the international law to accept and protect refugees. As with the ancient Greeks, in Japan strangers, *marebito* or "wandering persons", were fearsome, but were treated well

1 | http://www.etymonline.com/index.php?term=host (accessed 10 July 2012)

because they might be gods in disguise (Chapter 1; Ohnuki-Tierney, 1993). In most societies, hospitality to outsiders is a sign of generosity, wealth and good behaviour that raises one's prestige.

The rules of gift exchange and hospitality have been examined by Sahlins (1972), following Mauss (1967). The key concept is reciprocity – what people (or groups) owe to each other and the performance of acts of exchange over time is what holds communities together. Reciprocity is the basic human morality of exchange – of care, love, support, protection, sustenance and gifts – which should be balanced between friends or generalised (uncalculated) among close kin. Sahlins extends the concept to the human dimensions of market economies, which are based on *negative* reciprocity; but he shows that market and non-market transactions fall along a continuum in today's commercial world.

To repay an obligation is to perpetuate the relationship, and *not* to repay is to terminate or change it. For couchsurfers, to accept the guest into one's home is to continue the relationship with both the person *and* the institution, but to refuse them is to weaken or end it. The Christian story about Joseph and Mary being refused at the inn, so that Jesus was born in a stable, is a powerful parable about hospitality. The key to sustainable reciprocity is *time*. According to Lévi-Strauss (1949), immediate reciprocity – like paying with cash – cancels the debt and ends the alliance. But to lend something or to host someone creates a debt to be repaid in the future; when it is repaid the exchange is completed and that might be the end, but if the exchange is not exact – if the borrower pays back more than the debt or the host gives more lavish hospitality, for example – then this creates another debt that keeps the relationship going. Among the North West Coast Indians this was taken to extremes with a kind of competitive hospitality called *Potlatch* (Mauss 1967). Lévi-Strauss emphasized the "long cycle", like a chain where A owes to B, B to C, C to... and so on, to where X owes back to A, just as couchsurfers are a network of never-ending reciprocity.

Equality and alterity

Many of the chapters bring up the paradox of couchsurfers requiring their hosts to be culturally different but personally compatible. How can people be satisfactorily "the same" and "different"? Even the highly educated anthropologists have to find commonalities and understandings among the people where they are guests. And I have shown elsewhere (Graburn, 1983) that in spite of the emphasis on change, ritual inversion and alterity, tourists rarely wish to change more than a few of their routine situations, such as to accommodate more flexible schedules, better climate, more interesting people, foods and scenery, and their intellectual predilections, political affinities, sexual orientation or basic cultural tastes not at all. And so, with visitors choosing hosts (and to some extent vice versa) they look for "versions of themselves" within the same class stratum of their own or another society (Chapter 2).

This temporary society of former strangers is expected to result in closeness and familiarity, and is "impression-managed" according to stereotypes and trust. These "strangers on a train"-like meetings are exciting and provide for quick introductions of managed exoticism, along with customised hominess (Wang, 2007) and performative solidarity. The case studies relate situations where there are conflicts of hospitality regimes, which in turn provide for learning what are presumed to be cosmopolitan expectations. The cumulative result is the homogenisation of an "international middle class" comparable to academics or business people, which further distinguishes them from their less travelled peers at home.

PRECURSORS AND PARALLELS OF COUCHSURFING

I agree with Nash (1981) that is possible to identify aspects of "leisure travel" – traditional hosting and visiting – among such people as the Canadian Inuit. The term *pulaktuk* means "visits" someone, usually within the camp or village, but it was equally applied to visiting people in other communities for social purposes, different from *maqaituk* – "leaves home to go hunting". Much travel was undertaken to vary one's diet or to procure important materials or food when one's own area was depleted. Inuit voluntary travel-visiting always involved seeing friends and relatives (VFR); for men, it involved looking for temporary sex partners or future wives (if their own camp-mates were close relatives). Women rarely travelled without their male kin for either social or practical purposes. Like couchsurfing, arrival at a distant camp involved visual recognition and the exchange of stories of prior connections, mindful of negative possibilities of strangers' raids for women, food or equipment. Then the visitors would be invited for a meal and to stay in the tent or igloo, unless a large family made their own nearby.

Often single men were offered sexual hospitality (Graburn, 1969) – usually the host's wife, without her objection, an offer that should be reciprocated when the hosts in turn visited the guests, something which is nowhere mentioned in this volume.[2]

Although my anthropological travels through Inuit lands (24 villages since 1959) did not bear indigenous social or economic equality, arriving in a strange camp or village would require mechanisms of trust, for in many ways my life was in their hands. Often I travelled by dog sled, snowmobile or boat with Inuit friends who could "guarantee me". But arriving in my own, I would try to visit the relatives of friends elsewhere, and have something to offer: my knowledge of the language, Inuit genealogies and local histories, and my repertoire of traditional stories made me an "entertainer" who was encouraged to stay. Sometimes I brought hand-written letters from other villages and introduced myself as I delivered them (and carried answers or others on onward journeys). After community radio was introduced (in the 1980s) I would call-in messages asking for a host and give my sociocultural and personal credentials, much like the CS web site (Chapter 7). But the "leap of faith" required of me and my hosts was perhaps more like the cases of Tunisia, Taiwan or Viet Nam (chapters 1, 4, 5, 6), where there were profound cultural differences, and my personal "impression management" was geared to "Inuit cosmopolitanism" rather than the Western upper-middle class kind (cf. Chapter 2).

Aspects of contemporary couchsurfing were found in the flood of long distance youth travel in the 1960s and 1970s, an era of rebellion not only against workaday routines "*metro, boulot, dodo*" (subway-job-sleep) but against the parental generation's organised mass tourism. Sociologist Cohen (1973) describes this "moratorium on adulthood" of youth travelling to exotic places and with hopes of contact with nostalgic folksy cultures, foods and clothing, while ex-participant Teas (1988) emphasises the travellers' internal cultural competition over travelling, like Ramon (Chapter 2), as cheaply as possible for as long as possible, but with only symbolic (souvenir) contacts with indigenous peoples. These themes were later institutionalised in Japan and then China with TV shows about who could travel the furthest on the least cash, making friends with and relying on local hosts. Now this is even further commercialised by companies arranging "gap

2 | Surely some couchsurfing hosts might suggest a local brothel or a willing local girl or boy, or a wild party?

year" flights and finding hosts and NGO jobs in Third-world countries! For those new to couchsurfing, these intense experiences are self-imposed rites of passage comparable studying abroad, to long-distance backpacking or even "tours of duty" in military service (Carter, 2007). The "improving the world" goal expressed by many serious couchsurfers (see Chapter 1) is reminiscent of the 1960s Civil Rights activists in SNCC (the Student Nonviolent Coordinating Committee), who travelled to and in the US South and stayed (often on couches) with local people to assist with demonstrations, desegregation efforts and voter registration. The US Peace Corps started by President Kennedy (1961) shares many of the same themes of inter-cultural travel and living, with little or no pay, working for the good of local people. And today's solidarity and philanthropy tourism, to such places as Bosnia, Bolivia, Haiti, Afghanistan, Cuba and South Africa, share some of these features too, along with the tendency to become institutionalised by NGOs (e.g. Frères des Hommes, www.voluntourism.org).

Discussion

In the above accounts, we have seen that the struggle between the moral high-ground of non-commercial, generalised and balanced reciprocity versus institutional and commercial forms of hospitality still goes on. In a strange, nostalgic combination of semi-institutionalised reciprocity in the re-tribalised "global village", which McLuhan (1962) described as electronic interdependence,[3] the most highly educated use the most sophisticated technology to recreate pre-commercial ephemeral socialities (cf. Foster, 1986), hopefully characterised by ritual *communitas* (Graburn, 1983). Yet, this ritual bonding of equals (Turner, 1969) exaggerates differences, and mutual impression-management often leads to the hardening of stereotypes (cf. Laxson, 1991).

Historical contexts also show that market and non-market dimensions of human economies cannot be completely separated (Stertl, 2012). Some non-profit and friendship forms of hospitality, such as Home Exchange and Couchsurfing.org, are threatened by the temptation to become profit-making (chapters 1 and 2), much as hosts fear that guests are merely using

3 | McLuhan also coined the term "surfing" to refer to rapid movements through a body of documents or knowledge in a "tribal" acoustic space (Coupland, 2010).

them to provide a free bed (Chapter 3). There is a tendency for patterns of personal travels and hospitality to become more organised and commercialised (gap years, solidarity tours) as they become more routine, translating human feelings into monetary forms.[4] And service businesses, especially hospitality enterprises such as AirBnB and HomeAway, play down their profit-making aims by tempering their relationship to the customers and making them transparent and more personal, more like those with friends and family. Amen!

References

Cohen, E. (1973) "Nomads from affluence: notes on the phenomenon of drifter-tourism". *International Journal of Comparative Sociology* 14(1-2):89-103.

Coupland, D. (2010) *Marshall McLuhan: you know nothing of my work!* New York: Atlas.

Foster, G. (1986) "South Seas cruise: a case study of a short-lived society". *Annals of Tourism Research* 13(2):215-238.

Graburn, N. (1969) *Eskimos without igloos.* Boston: Little, Brown.

Graburn, N. (1983) "The anthropology of tourism". *Annals of Tourism Research* 10(1):9-33.

Laxson, J. (1991) "How 'we' see 'them': *tourism* and Native Americans". *Annals of Tourism Research* 18:374-375.

Leach, E. (1974) *Claude Lévi-Strauss.* New York: Viking Press.

Lévi-Strauss, C. (1949) *Les structures elémentaires de la parenté* (*Elementary Systems of Kinship*). Paris: Presses Universitaires de France.

Mauss, M. (1967 [1925]) *The gift: forms and functions of exchange in archaic societies.* New York: Norton.

McLuhan, M. (1962) *The Gutenberg galaxy: the making of typographic man.* Toronto: University of Toronto Press.

Nash, D. (1981) "Tourism as an anthropological subject". *Current Anthropology* 22(5):461-481.

Ohnuki-Tierney, E. (1993) *Rice as self: Japanese identities through time.* Princeton, NJ: Princeton University Press.

4 | There are many parallels in modern life, for instance most divorce cases in the Western world.

Okeley, J. (1996) *Own and other culture*. London: Routledge.

Powdermaker, H. (1966) *Stranger and friend: the way of an anthropologist*. New York: W.W. Norton.

Sahlins, M. (1972) *Stone Age economics*. Chicago: Aldine-Atherton.

Stertl, W. (2012) "Review for travelers: the pros and cons of Couchsurfing and AirBnB". *Condé Nast Traveler*. September 2012.

Teas, J. (1988) "I'm studying monkeys – what do you do? Youth travelers in Nepal". *Kroeber Anthropology Society Papers* 67-68:35-41.

Turner, V. (1969) *The ritual process: structure and anti-structure*. Chicago: Aldine.

Wang, Y. (2007) "Customized authenticity begins at home". *Annals of Tourism Research* 34(3):789-804.

List of Contributors

Paula Bialski holds a PhD in Sociology from Lancaster University. Paula is currently a post-doctoral researcher at the Hafen City University in Hamburg, working on a research project about Low-Budget Urbanity. She is also a Research Fellow at the Centre for Mobilities Research (CeMore), Lancaster University, and a guest lecturer at the Center for Social Studies at the Polish Academy of Sciences in Warsaw.

Sonja Buchberger teaches at École Hotelière de Lausanne (EHL) and at the School of Oriental and African Studies (SOAS), University of London, where she is currently completing her doctorate in Social Anthropology. Her thesis is on notions of hospitality, friendship, love and cosmopolitanism among Tunisian and Moroccan couchsurfing members.

De-Jung Chen is a PhD candidate in the research group Geographies of Globalizations at the Amsterdam Institute for Social Science Research (AISSR) at the University of Amsterdam. Her main research interests are niche tourism, popular culture and urban lifestyle. She is currently completing her research on hospitality exchange tourism in Taiwan and the Netherlands.

Jennie Germann Molz is Assistant Professor of Sociology at the College of the Holy Cross in Worcester, Massachusetts, where she teaches and conducts research on topics of tourism mobilities, mobile technologies, cosmopolitanism and hospitality. She is the author of *Travel Connections: Tourism, Technology and Togetherness in a Mobile World* (2012), founding co-editor of the journal *Hospitality & Society* (Intellect) and co-editor of the book *Mobilizing Hospitality: The Ethics of Social Relations in a Mobile World* (2007).

Nelson Graburn is Professor Emeritus of Sociocultural Anthropology at the University of California at Berkeley. Educated in Natural Sciences and Anthropology at Cambridge, McGill and the University of Chicago, he has carried out ethnographic research with the Inuit and Naskapi of Canada, Alaska and Greenland since 1959, and in Japan (and East and Southeast Asia) since 1974. His recent research has focused on the study of art, tourism, museums and the expression and representation of identity, with work being carried out on contemporary tourism in Asia (specifically Japan and China).

David Picard holds a PhD in Anthropology from the University of La Réunion, and currently works as a Senior Researcher at the Centre for Research in Anthropology (CRIA) in Lisbon, Portugal. His publications include a research monograph, *Tourism, Magic and Modernity: Cultivating the Human Garden* (2011) and several co-edited books: *Festivals, Tourism and Social Change* (2006), *The Framed World: Tourism, Tourists and Photography* (2009) and *Emotion in Motion: Tourism, Affect and Transformation* (2012). He currently leads research projects on magic and modernity in Southwest Madagascar and on Antarctic tourism cultures.

Bernard Schéou is a lecturer at the University of Perpignan in France and a researcher at the *Centre d'études sur la mondialisation, les conflits, les territoires et les vulnérabilités* at the University of Versailles-Saint-Quentin-en-Yvelines. Major publications include *Du tourisme durable au tourisme équitable. Quelle éthique pour le tourisme de demain ?* (2009) and "Le tourisme solidaire communautaire à l'épreuve des illusions culturaliste et participative, l'exemple d'une expérience au Bénin", which appeared in 2012 in *Monde en Développement* 40(157).

Jun-E Tan is currently a doctoral candidate at Nanyang Technological University in Singapore. She holds a master's degree in Public Policy from the University of Malaya and a bachelor's degree in Information Systems from Universiti Tunku Abdul Rahman in Malaysia. Her research interests include trust in social media and blogs and Malaysian politics. She has co-authored a book with Wan Zawawi Ibrahim entitled *Blogging and Democratization in Malaysia – A New Civil Society in the Making* (2008).

Dennis Zuev is a Research Fellow at CIES-ISCTE in Lisbon, Portugal and an Associate Researcher at the Siberian Studies Centre at the Max Planck Institute for Social Anthropology, Germany. He is a vice-president (research) of the Thematic Group *Visual Sociology* of the International Sociological Association.

Index

M

N

O

P

R

S

T

U

W